2017

DETERMINED TO RESTORE

AMERICA'S GREATNESS

MIKE DUCHEINE

MD Publishing Co.

2/3/2017

THIS PAGE IS LEFT BLANK INTENTIONALLY

TABLE OF CONTENTS

Quotes

When the truth reaches the mass, it becomes impossible to govern by deception. (Mike Ducheine)

Anyone can go to school to learn to read, to become very good at solving math problems or to even become excellent at writing proses but no one can become educated by going to school. (My mother)

Ignorance is the most effective tool of destruction but naivete is an offspring which must be aborted. (Mike Ducheine)

Torture is a delusion bridge which leads to deception but fear of torture is the most effective path to insightful information (Mike Ducheine)

Copyrights

DEDICATION

This book is dedicated exclusively
to my wife for her unrelenting
support, her incredible patience,
her unlimited understanding and her
immeasurable and infinite love

Preface

This book was written, edited and
published by MD Publishing; the
objective is to provide some context
into Donald Trump's presidency.
Most Republicans – *constituents and
legislators in particular* - consider
Trump's presidency as an opportunity
to undo everything Obama, continuing
what they tried for eight years during
his presidency. They hope to succeed
this time with a president who might
be willing to go along with their
plan.

Although it might be necessary for Mr.
Trump to modify or even undo some of
Obama's policies, the new president

should not rubberstamp everything the Republican Legislators in the Houses want to accomplish; after all, the oath of office he took in January 20, 2017 is to serve the country, not a Party. Coincidentally, that should also be the primary task of the Legislators.

The book outlines each of Obama's major policies and discusses the areas where Donald Trump could implement changes; it also outlines the pros & the cons of the proposed changes. In each instance, the book looks into the current state of the policy and what it means for Mr. Trump to build on, improve or undo.

Let's Meet Trump

Donald Trump acquired the label

Birther-In-Chief in 2009 when he self-promoted to spearhead the birther movement.

What is a birther? The birther movement was born with the election of Barack Obama to the presidency of the United States. Summarily, the birther participants and/or promoters claimed that Barack Obama was not a legitimate president because, as they advanced, he was not born in the country.

Although to be born in the United
States is not a requirement to become
president but to have been born a US
citizen is, the birtherists either did
not understand the mechanic of
citizenship or were simply blinded by
their hatred for the first black
president. Regardless where Barack
Obama was born, he would have been
born a US citizen because his mother
was. For the record, Barack Obama was
born Barack Hussein Obama II August 4,
1961 in Honolulu, Hawaii, U.S.A.
Besides, before any individual is
accepted to bid for the presidency of
the United States, such individual
must meet three basic criteria, one of
which is to be an American born
citizen. Needless to speculate whether
Mr. Obama met those criteria.

So, it is difficult to know for sure
whether Donald Trump believed the

"crap" he was saying or he simply used the birther campaign to keep himself in the spotlight, something he seems unable to live without or away from. If one were to believe the anecdotes, he even posed as someone else to promote himself (or his brand). Whether it's genius or a self-aggrandizement' illness, it's a behavior which has always worked for him.

Could Donald Trump have predicted he would be the one to succeed Obama, the very individual he tried to delegitimize for eight years? Probably not. Although he 'took a stab at' the presidency before, Mr. Trump didn't express much interest during Obama's tenure. It's almost certain to advance that Donald Trump stayed away from running for public office because of the fear to lose. The fear of losing

(anything, to anyone) is probably
Donald Trump's biggest nightmare. So,
it was not out of political ambition
Mr. Trump had waged a campaign against
Obama.

Although his behavior benefitted the
Republican Party – *he was a great help
to undermining Obama's presidency* – it
was not a coordinated effort between
Mr. Trump and the GOP. In fact, if one
followed Donald Trump closely during
the Obama years in the Oval Office,
his comments towards the president
were mixed (some good, some bad). One
could almost attribute his many
statements to that of an individual
with multiple personalities, and he
probably is.

Mr. Trump did not miss any White House
Correspondents' Dinner – *except the
last one (2016) for obvious reason* –
although it was certain there would be
a joke which would mention him. He
would smirk at the joke but one would
never catch him smiling let alone
laughing. And yet, every year, he
would attend the White House
Correspondents' dinner, a calculated
move which helped keep the "Trump"
brand in the spotlight, even at the
cost of a joke about him by the

president or the comedian or both. No
one could ever tell whether he enjoyed
the joke; he never expressed any
opinion to the contrary. Sometimes, he
would bob his head to the right to the
left; other times, he would simply
shrug and smirk.

Whatever it was, it couldn't have been
his hatred for Obama; many others who
truly despised Obama had carefully
planned not to be in the same room as
the 44th president to avoid him and yet
many others would even leave the room
as quickly as possible to avoid having
to shake the president's hands. Donald
Trump never fell into the category of
those who hated the president to that
extreme. One would even say that
Donald Trump secretly admired Obama.
And yet, during his presidency, Mr.
Obama was antagonized by Donald Trump
on a regular basis.

One could reach the conclusion that Mr. Trump kept at it (the birther campaign) in order to prevent the spotlight from going away or being stolen by others.

Obama Birth Certificate

There were many others who had also advanced theories about Obama's birthplace. And everyone was fighting to scream the loudest, to make the most outrageous claim, to become the top conspiracy theorist. But it was Donald Trump who won and kept the title of birther-in-chief, an expression which was used by the Clinton's campaign in the 2016 presidential elections. Mr. Trump had upped the ante by voicing publicly every so often what he was doing to prove he was right all along about Obama's non-US citizenship. Mr. Trump became so persistent, - *he claimed he would provide proof that the president wasn't born in Hawaii* - that the White House decided to release Mr. Obama's birth certificate (picture above).

In a world other than Donald Trump's, that would have been the end of the birther movement; that would have been the end of the story about the president's birthplace. Not a chance said Donald, I have people looking into the matter to prove that the release of the president's birth certificate was smoke and mirrors. Unable to follow through with "the proof", Mr. Trump went underground for a while. A few months of silence from Donald Trump about that issue could have been interpreted that Mr. Trump had finally given up; he didn't. In fact, Mr. Trump bounced back with a new theory that would prove, as he claimed, he indeed knew the president wasn't born in the country; he demanded the president to release his college transcripts.

At this point, the White House had moved on and left Donald Trump completely naked in his campaign against the president's citizenship. Even Republican judges across the country had dismissed ALL of the cases brought to court in regards to that matter. However, to keep the issue alive and keep himself on the spotlight, Mr. Trump proposed a $10 million to a charitable organization in exchange for the White House to release Obama's college transcripts. His offer fell flat; there was no taker. His request sounded more like a rescue plea from a badly defeated previously "undefeatable" champion. He was again completely ignored. For a while, Mr. Trump stopped the birther dance and began to focus on more important matters, mainly to run for public office.

When he approached the GOP elites and powerbrokers, they quickly suggested that he ran for governor of New York to challenge then governor Mario Cuomo but Mr. Trump had a much bigger target in sight, the presidency of the United States. To the GOP elites, that was lunacy; so, they did what they've always done: they issued an ultimatum to Trump, take it or you're on your own. - *In hindsight, that was a big mistake on the part of the Republican elites; maybe not. After all, Trump would later reach out to most of them in the making of his cabinet.* - And Trump did what one would expect him to do, especially when challenged as the GOP did in that case, to work towards showing "them" he could make it, going it alone.

Trump moved away from the GOP powerbrokers; in fact, he stopped consulting with them altogether. As a businessman, Trump must think outside the box, and he did. Trump is forever conscious that the biggest obstacle to success is lack of motivation and self-confidence; and to become successful, one must rid of those who cannot dream big. And he has done just that in his business operation; Trump is famous for "firing" people who suggested that something could not be done. He had the drive, the determination, the will and most importantly money is no objection to the Donald.

When words got out that Donald Trump would consider a run for the presidency, no one paid much attention to the rumors; after all, Mr. Trump had threatened to bid for the presidency for quite some time. Donald Trump is on record exploring the possibility of a presidential run in 1987-88. That may have been a diversion – *something Trump has always been very good at* – since Trump had to deal with some very large debts stemming from the purchase of the Taj Mahal casino.

Time Magazine ran a piece to talk
about the successful businessman who
had turned his attention towards a
bigger prize, the White House

http://www.newsweek.com/rise-trump-357533

Needless to point out the obvious; it
didn't go well for Mr. Trump and his
ego.
Twelve years later however, in 2000,
Trump entered the presidential race as
a Reform Party candidate; it didn't go
well at all; in fact, he only got
15,000 votes from the state of

California. Such record is humiliating to Trump but one thing has always been true about Donald Trump, he always spends time to figure out why he failed at anything. He must have figured it out. He again considered a run for the presidency in 2003-2004 but abandoned the idea early on. In 2011-2012, after summoning the candidates for president (including Mitt Romney, Rick Santorum, Newt Gingrich, Herman Cain, Michele Bachman) to a live televised debate he would moderate failed, Mr. Trump went into a rampage, insulting all the candidates and threatened "to throw his hat into the ring" (running for the presidency); he accused them of being weak, of being unable to counter Obama. In the end, he abandoned the idea, settled down and provided a full throated endorsement to then GOP nominee Mitt Romney.

So, it was understandable that no one
paid much attention to the rumors that
Donald Trump was contemplating a run
for the presidency in 2015. However,
it appeared Mr. Trump was serious that
time around; it was not another one of
his acts or self-promotion. For
starter, he decided NOT to renew the
Apprentice contract, a very big deal.
Mr. Trump is not one to walk away from
money and the spotlight, unless there
is something else that would benefit
him more and keep the spotlight on him
longer. Well, there was. In June 2015,
at the Trump Tower in Manhattan,
Donald Trump, in a very trumpistic
way, announced his candidacy for the
presidency of the United States.
In full, is described below in an
article the day Donald Trump descended
the elevator to make the memorable and
historic announcement:

Donald Trump announcement as candidate for president is reminiscent of the Herman Cain 2012 presidential bid. It is funny, hilarious and downright entertaining. For starter, it is reported that Trump's campaign hired actors to attend his announcement, not just to hear about his vision for America but also to cheer him during the course of the announcement. Like most candidates who are not seasoned politicians, Mr. Trump started on the wrong foot; then again, maybe not. Mr. Trump is known for his extravaganzas, his boisterous behavior and his loose tongue; don't expect anything less. We probably all know that Mr. Trump is egocentric and doesn't back down from a fight; that may actually be a good thing for the Republican Party.

While comedians have been having the time of their lives since the announcement, and for good reason (see Jon Stewart talking about the Donald Trump announcement), Donald Trump addition to the long list of Republicans seeking the office of the presidency will not just be entertaining but will also force the other candidates to pay attention to the issues which matter to Trump and to address them. If we know one thing about Donald Trump, he is not one to walk away from a fight easily, usually; he is not one to accept losing. Although we predict Trump's campaign may be short lived, not for lack of financing, – during his announcement, Mr. Trump made it clear what his net worth is – but because Mr. Trump is a businessman first. He looks at everything he does in term of return on investment (ROI). To run for office, unless he could move up fast in the polls, doesn't have any immediate tangible return (financial or otherwise); if anything, this venture will take Mr. Trump away from making money, something he may not be able "to stomach" for long.

So, what should we expect from Donald Trump as a candidate?

Despite the ridicule endured by Mr. Trump since the announcement, one should not discard or minimize his influence in the debates on many issues. Any candidate who would dare to ignore, cross or attempt to sideline Mr. Trump would do it at his/her own peril. Love him, hate him, ridicule him, at least Mr. Trump makes a semblance of addressing issues (sort of) he cares about (which some constituents might too). Thus far, all other candidates have one common plan for the country, undo everything Obama has implemented (from Obamacare to

Foreign relations) without offering any logical or substantial alternative. This is the irony of election cycles in the country, nobody cares, not the politicians seeking office, not even the constituents who claim to be tired of Washington corruption, unwillingness and inability to fix any problem. With Mr. Trump in the mix, one can hope that his bombastic (truly unorthodox) approach to seeking the office of the presidency would gain enough attention (as if he has not yet) to force discussions of issues Mr. Trump would consider important for debate.

Watch how Mr. Trump will veer the discussion in the first debate – slated for August 6, 2015 at 9pm in New Hampshire – especially when asked questions he may have no clue what the answer should be. If history is any guide, Mr. Trump's rating (just like Herman Cain's in 2012) will go up fast (in flames), probably surpassing all others, an outcome that will surely fire up the Trump's campaign in anticipation of securing the nomination. However, it could become obvious to Mr. Trump that to run for office is a very taxing endeavor, the return is very fluid (if at all) and the candidate has no direct control over the outcome, something Mr. Trump may not be able to live with for long.

Without boring you through the ebbs and flows of the elections, suffice to say that Donald Trump had managed to outwit everybody: seasoned politicians, pollsters, pundits, political analysts, and yes even psychics to secure the GOP nomination and win the general election to become the 45th president of the United States.

Despite the controversies surrounding him, mainly the meddling of Russia into the election process, Donald was sworn in as the president and will have to attend to the task all presidents before him had. In general, every president walks into the Oval Office with one ultimate objective: to define, to craft a legacy. Every president hopes to be judged kindly by history but Donald Trump is no ordinary president. He has already proved it even in the choices of his cabinet; he ran a campaign against the political and financial fixtures in Washington. The slogan "drain the swamp" was meant to rid Washington of – *ultimately prevent his administration from* – all those elements which contributed to the status quo and the gridlock in Washington. Surprise! Surprise! His

cabinet comprises those very elements
he claimed he wanted to get rid of.

Mr. Trump is weird, obnoxious,
unpredictable but he does want to
craft his brand; that may be
sufficient to motivate him to do
what's good for the country but most
likely what's best for his brand,
hopefully also good for the country.
To that end, Mr. Trump should continue
to use the same strategy which has
served him well in his business
activities. Although each president is
tempted to undo most everything his
predecessor (of the other party) has
accomplished, Donald Trump should
resist the urge to do so, especially
considering the political climate:
Republicans are a majority in both
Houses. Mr. Trump must learn quickly
to understand that the presidency of
the United States is not a sport game

where one individual or one party tries to score against the other once it has the ball.

If Mr. Trump truly wants to "Make America Great Again", he needs to focus his attention to crafting his own legacy, something which cannot be achieved by trying to destroy someone else's, Obama's. It is quite possible that his plan for the country may require to undo some of what Obama has accomplished but it's bad governance to specifically target Obama's achievement either in retaliation for something he said or simply because he is a Democrat. The country needs to move forward; that cannot happen if every time a party occupies the Oval Office, the mission becomes a "destroy the previous administration" achievements.

It is widely expected that Donald Trump may not necessarily go along with everything the Republicans in the Houses have in mind. As a "successful" businessman, Donald Trump learned very early on from his father to build on others' success. That's what Donald Trump did; he built on his father's success. So, it would be foolish for him to believe that one can simply shoot for the star bypassing everything which was previously built. To follow Mr. Trump in his journey to Make America Great Again, we must look back into what his predecessor had accomplished in order to assess what Mr. Trump may need to do and where he could improve on, change or completely undo some of the predecessor's policies in order to achieve something better for the country.

Let's roll!

This page is left blank intentionally

Obama's Presidency

Since his inauguration in 2009, the president had not received any support from any Republican Legislator in Washington. This was unprecedented.

Although it is common practice that party affiliation determines the level of support (how much or how little) a president would receive from the Legislators of the opposing party, it is however extremely unusual that a sitting president would have so little cooperation from the Representatives of the opposing Party.

While it seems obvious by most analysis that the main factor was the president's race, it is worth noting that the President had also adopted a "non-mingling" approach vis-à-vis the GOP Lawmakers in Washington.

Be it by design or simply because of the environment the Republicans had created, the president style was also a factor in the final outcome of the relation. It probably would not have mattered anyway; in fact, from the very beginning, the Republican Legislators drew a line in the sand; they were very forthcoming in their agenda, to deny the president a second term, hardly a good way to jumpstart a new relationship.

Everything Republicans in Washington had done was to challenge the president not just in political sense; they had questioned his citizenship, they had attacked his patriotism; they had questioned his motives, his love for the country. As such, anyone can

easily conclude that Mr. Obama had
held the office of the presidency
under extremely challenging
circumstances.

The following discussion is twofold:
1) an attempt to provide a factual
account of Obama' presidency by
discussing a few of his
accomplishments and failures.
2) analysis of the effectiveness of
each policy and whether it warrants
president Trump to build on, improve,
modify or completely undo

The Meaning of Obama

If you were to come from another planet and visited Earth between January 2009 and the year 2016 and the first broadcast station you tune in to on your visit to the planet is Fox Opinion, – *known and referred to by most as Fox News* – the word Obama, the expression Barack Obama (and any derivation) would have probably meant "complete failure", "utmost evil", "despicable organism" or simply "irritating parasite". According to Fox Opinion, Obama presidency has been a disaster, much, much worse than that of George W. Bush, the 43rd president of the United States.

Seriously!

If there was anything remotely good or positive which had happened under the Obama administration, it must have been inevitable; something which would have happened anyway, irrespective of the occupant in the Oval Office. In other words, according to Fox Opinion, if it was bad, Obama was responsible; if it was good, Obama could not claim credit because it was probably a fluke, an anomaly. But Fox Opinion failed short to point out that "Evil King Obama" had managed to seduce a whole nation, well, most of the nation (the world even) to accept him as commander-in-chief of the most powerful nation on earth, the United States of America. Hosts at Fox implied that Obama had managed not just to be elected but also to be re-elected despite being a foreigner.

God forbid!

The GOP mouthpiece (Fox Opinion) may
have been on to something but a few
details its hosts might have
overlooked are discussed below in
order to provide a more complete
picture regarding the extent of the
failure of the Obama presidency (*or
his accomplishments if one doesn't
work at Fox*).

On the Spotlight

Whenever an important issue such as
terrorism arose, one was certain to
hear many different views and opinions
on how best to handle the aftermath of
a tragedy such as the Brussels'
airport attacks (http://bbc.in/2eboq8b) on
March 22, 2016.

The opinions were usually framed
according to the political party the
individuals belonged to. In other
words, you'd be hard pressed to hear
any objective analysis of those types
of situation. Each party wanted to
discuss these topics in such a way to
score political points, especially in
an election cycle such as the 2016
presidential election season we were
in (*at the time of the writing of this
book*) even if it meant that the
country would not benefit from their
arguments. So, it should not surprise
anyone to hear many different views,
opinions and commentaries regarding
not only the Brussel's terrorist
attacks but also how president Obama
handled or reacted to the tragedies.

That's where I come in. As I mentioned
frequently in *The People Branch* blog
(http://peoplebranch.org), I have no allegiance

to any political party or candidate which frees me to be more or less objective in all matter politics. This is not to say one would agree with everything I write about; this is not to imply that I am 100% bias free. Far from it! I am still human, you know. However, because I am not in a race to please one party or the other, one candidate or another, one group or another, I can be more objective than most.

Having said that, I will take a look at how Republicans and Democrats have judged Obama vis-à-vis his legacy in general and the tragedies of terrorism in particular which have thus far claimed the lives of hundreds and injured thousands here and abroad during his eight years in office.

I will also look at the devastation of terrorist actions (here and abroad), their aftermath and Obama's reactions through three different prisms, the Republican's, the Democrat's and the Objective's (*which is neither Republican nor Democrat*). Let's get to it.

The Republican Prism

Contrary to the Republican Party in general, Donald Trump used to speak highly of Obama. In his 2009 book "Think Like a Champion", Trump wrote that what Obama *"has done is amazing...the fact that he accomplished what he has - in one year and against great odds - is truly phenomenal."* Trump believed that Obama had *"the mark of a strong leader"* with an understanding of the economy.

He related the fact in the book this way *"As of October of 2008, the US Government reported a $237 billion deficit. The good news is that Obama seems to be well aware of the situation. His comments led me to believe that he understands how the economy works on a comprehensive level. He has also surrounded himself*

with very competent people, and that's the mark of a strong leader.
I have confidence he will do his best, and we have someone who is serious about resolving the problems we have and will be facing in the future."
In addition, during an interview with Larry King at CNN on April 2009, Mr. Trump commented that *"the world looks at us differently than they used to"* because of Obama. But as you will read below, Donald Trump's view of Obama was starkly different from the Republican Party.

Obama is probably the worst president in modern time; as the first black president, Mr. Obama is a disgrace to the Black community. Minority is worse off under Obama than any other president in recent memory. The country is worse off than when he took office; he implemented policies which do not align with American values; his immigration policy is the worst of all time, he has allowed 11 million illegal immigrants in the country; he made a deplorable nuclear deal agreement with Iran; he doesn't support our friend and ally Israel; he jeopardized freedom of religion; he has stifled freedom of speech. The country has lost respect overseas. Libya is now a mess; Syria is in shambles. All in all, Obama's presidency is much, much worse than George W. Bush.

What you just read is an autopsy of the Obama administration by the Republican Party.

It is a very foggy prism to look through when it comes to Obama. Since he's occupied the Oval Office, there was never a single word Mr. Obama had

uttered or a single action he had
taken or a single move he had made
which was considered good by the
Republicans. You can understand the
dilemma, can't you?

Even if one were to be the most stupid
individual on the planet, there could
be times when that "idiot" would do
something or say something, even
despite himself, which would be good,
let alone a Harvard graduate, an
accomplished Senator, a calculated
politician and now the president of
the most powerful country on earth.
You can appreciate the dilemma, can't
you?

If you tune in to any broadcaster or
entertainer in the GOP camp (Sean
Hannity and company at Fox, Rush
Limbaugh (who doesn't know Rush?),
Glenn Beck and the whole gang of

Republican broadcasters, reporters, journalists, opinion writers, commentators, etc.), Obama's presidency has been a disaster was usually the rallying theme.

Even what appeared to be (or was) good such as a low unemployment rate was attributed to something other than Obama's policy or actions his administration had taken to tackle the high unemployment problem or any other issue he inherited when he took office. In other words, Obama had not, did not and could not do anything which was right when looked through the Republican Prism.

It should not be any surprise to you (or anyone else) that his reactions in regards to the Airport tragedies in Brussels caused by terrorism were also wrong, inappropriate. Printed everywhere Republican, he should have done this, he should have done that, he should have done the other.

The Republican candidates vying for the Oval Office jumped on the bandwagon to give their two-cents opinion, and if you guessed that they thought the president didn't react appropriately or accordingly, you must be a psychic.

John Kasich suggested he would have ended whatever he was doing at the time, turned Air Force One around to go back to Washington. Hmm! Suffice to say that the president of the United States is always in office no matter where he's at. Coincidentally, Air Force One was built as a mobile office for the President of the United States. The plane is equipped with the most sophisticated technology. For the president of the United States NOT to be physically in the Oval Office does not change any aspect of his job as president. John Kasich of all people – *he was a politician in Washington who had not only spent a great deal of time there but also ran for president twice (2000 and 2016), was considered as running mate by Bob Dole (1996), met with Ronald Reagan in the Oval Office and learned a great deal about the presidency* – should know that the President is abreast of any situation no matter where he is at in the world. So, the call to "turn Air Force One around" was at best cheap political shots. Well, I did say we were looking at Obama's presidency through the Republican prism, didn't I?

The Democrat Prism

As it should become obvious very
quickly, Donald Trump's views on Obama
in the beginning were more aligned
with the Democrats than they were with
the Republicans'

Looking through the Democrat Prism is
somewhat less foggy albeit slightly
less biased than the Republican's,
understandably so; Democrats tend to
be more independently minded and very
diverse in their opinions in regards
to their Party in general and the
president in particular. Some
Democrats believed the President
reacted appropriately in regards to
the Brussels Airport explosions,
continuing whatever course he was in;
other Democrats thought he should have
handled the news of the tragedy
differently.

As it might already be obvious, Democrats are usually more inclined to strike a balance, be it about a Democratic or a Republican President. As such, the president's reactions to the terrorist actions in Belgium were met with mixed reactions in the Democrat camp. For instance, contrary to Republicans who saw everything George W. Bush did – *including misleading the country about the existence of weapon of mass destruction (WMD) in Iraq in order to take the country to war or even his handling of the Katrina* (http://bit.ly/2itVpnt) *aftermath, one of the most devastating hurricane which hit the region in 2005* – when he was in office as good but whatever Obama had done as bad or wrong, both Tom Brokaw and Chris Matthews of MSNBC (*a Democrat leaning network*) lambasted

Obama for "not acting like a leader".
Tom Brokaw angrily uttered "Time to be
the leader" and proceeded to recite a
list of terrorist actions which have
happened since September 11, 2001; -
*it was not clear whether Mr. Brokaw
tried to pin the blame on Obama for
terrorism before his presidency by
referring to those instances of
terrorism* - Chris Matthews thought
that "Obama Off Base in response to
Brussels' attacks, you don't want to
hear he phoned it in". And of course
there were many legislators and
members of his cabinet who came out to
his defense, rightfully so; that was
their primary task, to support and
defend their boss.

The contrast presented above does not
represent an acknowledgement that the
diverse reactions by the Democrats
vis-à-vis the president regarding the

terrorist actions at the Brussels' Airport (*or any other similar situation*) were correct or appropriate. Both criticism and support could be off base, for the public does not have the relevant information the President of the United States uses to make decisions. The aforementioned example only serves to outline the contrast between Democrats and Republicans in general.

Obama A Political Houdini

Some analysts are inclined to refer to
Barack Obama as a political Houdini.

Harry Houdini, an early 20th century
magician, is believed to have
performed sensational escape acts
which have defied logic. Most of his
magic acts consisted having both his
hands and feet cuffed and chained
(sometimes in straight jacket) and
dropped under water. He would manage

to free himself and emerge above water unscathed. His most daring act was to be buried alive, leaving just enough room so he could claw his way out from the grave should he survive; well, he did.

Without the entertainment aspect of the escape acts, Barack Obama had managed to put Harry Houdini to shame. While Houdini's acts were believed to be staged (*which most likely were*), Obama never had the luxury to perform illusory acts on his audience:

a) the recession was not fake and could not be staged when he took office
b) the Wall Street fallout was not staged when he took office
c) the auto industry in shambles was not staged when he took office
d) the mounting deficit could not be staged when he took office

e) the mounting debt was not fake
   when he took office
f) the million dollar daily cost of
   the ongoing wars in Iraq &
   Afghanistan was not an act when
   he took office
g) the high unemployment rate was
   not staged when he took office.

But the modern day political Houdini
Barack Obama, with both hands and feet
chained by the Republican led House
and the Senate, managed to free
himself and accomplished what was
perceived as impossible to do even
without the restrictions.
Put differently, Barack Obama
performed the greatest magic act never
attempted by any politician on the
planet, a daring escape not even Harry
Houdini could have achieved.
To a great degree, Donald Trump
decided to bid for the presidency of

the United States because he was
highly inspired by Obama and
mesmerized at the fact that a black
man, a junior Senator could overcome
so many obstacles to become the
president of the United States, a
country which still has a very large
population of White nationalists.

The Objective Prism

Because human bias cannot be
completely eliminated, most analysis
would usually reflect that fact;
however, if one is rational and
genuinely wants to form an objective
opinion about something or someone, it
is still possible. Here I will attempt
to submit opinions based almost
exclusively on analysis of facts,
events and circumstances; I will try
as best as possible to avoid

discussing my preferences or to even judge others' (No promise). My primary objective is to let the facts do the talking. Here we go!

On the historic day of the inauguration of Barack Obama as first black president of the United States, a few blocks away, the Republican elites, powerbrokers and legislators gathered, not to celebrate or even acknowledge history but to devise a plan on how best to make Obama's presidency a blip, an irrelevancy at best but a disastrous one nevertheless. The very next day, Senate Majority Leader, Republican Representative Mitch McConnell from Kentucky publicly outlined his most important agenda: to make Barack Obama a one-term president regardless the cost and the consequences (*to the country and its citizens*).

Mitch wasn't joking; it wasn't politics as usual. His statement was crafted after a series of discussions and deliberations overnight with GOP leaders and powerbrokers during the president's inauguration. Without the need to re-hash the Republican House performance during Obama's presidency, Senator Mitch McConnell worked hard to make good on his promise. Rush Limbaugh – *a Republican idealist broadcaster/entertainer* – expressed in one sentence what the Republican Legislators set out to do: "I hope the president fails".

Coincidentally, most Republican and Republican leaning individuals share Mitch's ideals; they had all helped him along the way; in addition to creating the "Birther" Movement, the gist of which was to claim that Barack

Obama was not born in the United States and there was proof to back up the claim. Apparently, the only purpose for the existence of the Birther movement was to delegitimize Obama as president; per the United States Constitution, the individual seeking the office of the presidency must be born in the country. One cannot under any circumstance assume the office of the presidency if that individual acquired the American citizenship through naturalization. So, by claiming that Obama was not born in the United States was to indirectly state that he was not eligible to become president in the first place. The "Birthers" went as far as to file papers with the court to have Obama removed from office; they had insulted him regularly, they opposed everything he attempted to do to move the country forward.

Rush Limbaugh – *a man who needs no introduction* – summed up the feeling of the Republicans (*voters and leaders alike*) towards Obama at the time: I hope the president fails he said on his daily radio show shortly after Obama assumed the presidency. Here is in essence what president Obama had to deal with during his presidency: a concerted effort to oppose everything he tried to do, an irrational call for him to fail. It was the first time in the history of the presidency that a president did not have a single ally on any policy from the opposing party.

Most Republicans were quick to dismiss the idea that the president's race was factored in their extreme position. For over two hundred years, politics has always been bad, ugly, nasty even but history had never recorded such extreme position taken by the opposing party towards a president, until Obama that is. Was it just a coincidence that the first black president was treated just like any other black (*with disrespect*)? Irrespective of what it was, Barack Obama had not only soared above the fray – *he took the high road* – but he had managed to get a lot done during his presidency despite all obstacles laid on his (political) path by the Republicans. It is worth mentioning here again that Donald Trump was one of the most vocal and outspoken individuals pushing the birther movement into the national stage. It is impossible to figure out even as of date whether his intentions went beyond staying in the spotlight.

Below, I discuss some of the most important items Obama had on his agenda when he took office in January

2009 and how he has fared with just a few months away from the end of his presidency.

This page is intentionally left blank

FOREIGN POLICY

Republicans like to argue against facts in general, in reference to Obama in particular; as such, it should not surprise anyone to hear Republicans' reflection that the country was in much worse shape under Obama than it was under George W. Bush, and U.S. standing in the world stage was at its lowest since Obama took office. Unsurprisingly, Fox Opinion – *known and referred to by most as Fox News* – bears a major portion of the blame. Most Republicans tune in almost exclusively to Fox' programs which support their ideals and beliefs, however fact free those programs are. To every host at Fox, Obama did not and could not possibly have done anything good or right.

On Tuesday, June 2nd 2015, Gretchen Carlson, host at Fox said this:

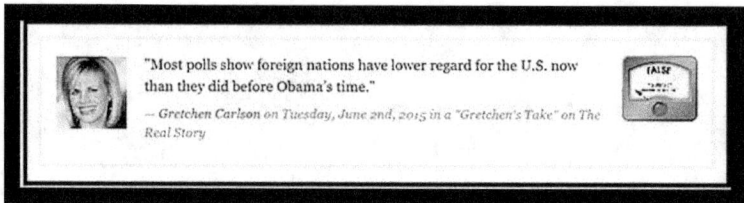

"Most polls show foreign nations have lower regard for the U.S. now than they did before Obama's time."
— *Gretchen Carlson on Tuesday, June 2nd, 2015 in a "Gretchen's Take" on The Real Story*

a statement that was proven to be completely false according to Politifact.com. US standing in the world during the Bush administration is best explained by then President of Venezuela, Hugo Chavez. In his speech at the United Nations in 2006, he referred to President Bush as "the devil" who thinks he is "the owner of the world."

"Yesterday, the devil came here. Right here. Right here. And it smells of sulfur still today, this table that I am now standing in front of." Mr. Chavez said to the General Assembly.

One doesn't need Politifact or any other facts check organization to know that U.S. standing in the world could not possibly have been worse under Obama than it was under George W. Bush. After alienating US main allies such as France, Spain, Italy, Germany, the Bush administration had adopted an arrogant posture towards them even in the face of revelations which proved that the world was misled by his administration. Here at home, the verdict – *to deal with such blatant deception* - was swift and decisive; the election of Barack Obama, a junior Senator with no foreign policy experience over John McCain, a war hero, a politician and an individual with foreign policy experience settled the matter that the electorate would not be happy with another Republican president in the Oval Office. It should have been obvious to the

political strategists and the Bush
administration advisors in general and
the Republican powerbrokers in
particular that when the truth reaches
the mass it becomes impossible to
govern and to lead by deception.

Contrary to George W. Bush, the Obama
administration' approach to the world
was conciliatory, something which had
angered the Republicans - applauded by
Donald Trump - who had accused Obama
regularly of being a weak president.
His speech in Cairo, Egypt on June 4,
2009, just six months into his
presidency, was an olive branch
extended to the Arabs, a major
departure from the previous
administration whose primary policy
was to wage wars against Muslims and
beyond.

Obama's attempt to reconcile the United States with the Arab world was not without drawbacks; such approach created friction between the United States and the State of Israel, a conundrum his administration had operated under and around for the major part of his presidency. A nuclear deal agreement with Iran (http://wp.me/p1yu17-mR) – *a positive step to end Iran' nuclear ambitions by any analysis* – contributed to exacerbate the friction between US and Israel, the latter having publicly and vehemently opposed the nuclear agreement. The rest of the world community however saw those overtures by the Obama administration as the right approach.

It is worth note here that Donald Trump shares most of Mr. Obama's position vis-à-vis the Israeli-Palestine conflicts; however, during the general elections, he was pressured by the Republicans (and the Republican Party) to take a public stance which favors Israel.

On the world stage, US has regained some level of prestige which was badly damaged during the Bush years, an observation Mr. Trump made during an interview accorded to CNN host Larry King. As shown in the graph below provided by Pew Research Center, European nations gave US a higher approval "to do the right thing" rating (*more than 20 points by Spain & Germany, more than 30 points by France and UK*) under Obama than under the Bush administration.

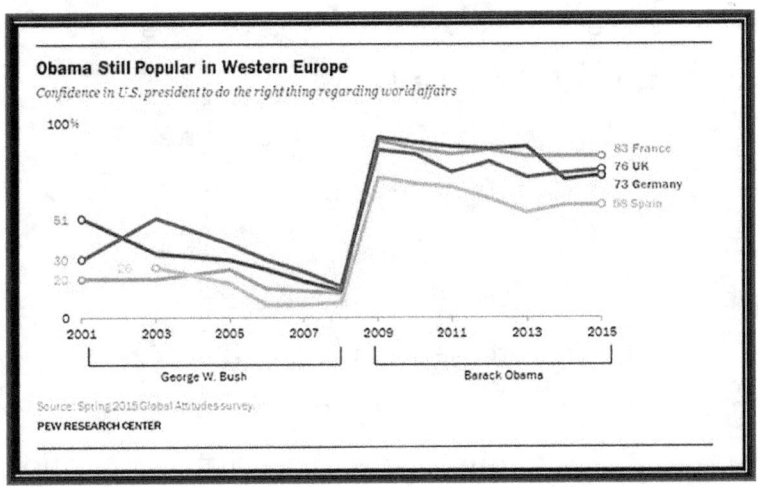

So, it is difficult if not impossible to imagine that US standing on the world stage could be worse under Obama than it was under George W. Bush. In addition to having adopted a non-bully approach in foreign policy, the Obama administration had worked diligently to open the doors of relations with countries which were once considered US enemies.

For instance, in a major reversal of US policy towards Cuba, Obama negotiated through diplomatic back-channels with Canada serving as intermediary the lifting of the embargo on Cuba. On March 21-22 2014, on the backdrop of Cuban exiled protests on the streets of Miami, Florida, Obama (and his family) took a trip to Havana, Cuba to meet with Raoul Castro the president of Cuba and visit historic sites. And on August 31, 2016, the first US commercial flight in more than 50 years landed on Cuban soil.

Obama also visited Argentina in a move to bury the hatchet between the United States and Argentina. Argentinians have always been suspicious of Washington, and for good reason. They have decried US hypocrisy waging wars in the name of democracy. Argentinians were subjected to tortures and mass executions in the "dirty war" under dictator Pinochet whose government was initially supported by the US government.

Obama's visit to Argentina was to allay the concerns of the Argentinians and reiterate US commitment to human rights; as a gesture of good faith towards the Argentinian government and its people, Obama proposed to de-classify documents related to the periods of US relations with dictator Pinochet. Those overtures by the Obama administration contributed to elevate US standing in the world. The chart below provides a glimpse of how much Obama foreign policy has impacted the US standing on the world stage over the years.

U.S. Favorability	Under George W. Bush								Under Barack Obama						
	1999/2000	2002	2003	2004	2005	2006	2007	2008	2009	2010	2011	2012	2013	2014	2015
	%	%	%	%	%	%	%	%	%	%	%	%	%	%	%
Canada	–	72	63	–	59	–	55	–	68	–	–	–	64	–	68,
France	62	62	42	37	43	39	39	42	75	73	75	69	64	75	73
Germany	78	60	45	38	42	37	30	31	64	63	62	52	53	51	50
Italy	76	70	60	–	–	–	53	–	–	–	–	74	76	78	83
Poland	86	79	–	–	62	–	61	68	67	74	70	69	67	73	74
Spain	50	–	38	–	41	23	34	33	58	61	64	58	62	60	65
UK	83	75	70	58	55	56	51	53	69	65	61	60	58	66	65
Russia	37	61	37	46	52	43	41	46	44	57	66	52	51	23	15
Ukraine	–	–	–	–	–	–	–	–	–	–	–	–	–	68	69
Turkey	52	30	15	30	23	12	9	12	14	17	10	15	21	19	29
Jordan	–	25	1	5	21	15	20	19	25	21	13	12	14	12	14
Lebanon	–	36	27	–	42	–	47	51	55	52	49	48	47	41	39
Palest. ter.	–	–	0	–	–	–	13	–	15	–	18	–	16	30	26
Israel	–	–	78	–	–	–	78	–	71	–	72	–	83	84	81
Australia	–	–	59	–	–	–	–	46	–	–	–	–	66	–	63
China	–	–	–	–	42	47	34	41	47	58	44	43	40	50	44
India	–	–	–	–	–	–	–	–	–	–	–	–	56	55	70
Indonesia	–	–	–	–	38	30	29	37	63	59	54	–	61	59	62
Japan	77	72	–	–	–	63	61	50	59	66	85	72	69	66	68
Malaysia	–	–	–	–	–	–	27	–	–	–	–	–	55	51	54
Pakistan	23	10	–	21	23	27	15	19	16	17	12	12	11	14	22
Philippines	–	90	–	–	–	–	–	–	–	–	–	–	85	92	92
South Korea	58	52	46	–	–	–	58	70	78	79	–	–	78	82	84
Vietnam	–	–	–	–	–	–	–	–	–	–	–	–	–	76	78
Argentina	50	34	–	–	–	–	16	22	38	42	–	–	41	36	43
Brazil	–	–	–	–	–	–	–	–	–	62	62	61	73	65	73
Chile	–	–	–	–	–	55	–	–	–	–	–	–	68	72	68
Mexico	68	64	–	–	–	–	56	47	69	56	52	56	66	63	66
Peru	74	67	–	–	–	–	61	–	–	–	–	–	–	65	70
Venezuela	–	–	–	–	–	–	–	–	–	–	–	–	53	62	51
Burkina Faso	–	–	–	–	–	–	–	–	–	–	–	–	–	–	79
Ethiopia	–	–	–	–	–	–	–	–	–	–	–	–	–	–	81
Ghana	–	83	–	–	–	80	–	–	–	–	–	–	83	77	89
Kenya	94	80	–	–	–	87	–	–	90	94	83	–	81	80	84
Nigeria	–	–	–	–	–	–	–	–	–	81	–	–	69	69	76
Senegal	–	–	–	–	–	–	–	–	–	–	–	–	81	74	80
South Africa	–	65	–	–	–	–	–	60	–	–	–	–	72	68	74
Tanzania	–	53	–	–	–	–	46	65	–	–	–	–	–	75	78
Uganda	–	74	–	–	–	–	64	–	–	–	–	–	73	62	76

Note: 1999/2000 survey trends provided by the U.S. Department of State.

Source: Spring 2015 Global Attitudes survey. Q126

PEW RESEARCH CENTER

The column on the left of the chart shows US Standing on the world under George W. Bush in his first year in office; as it is evident, Canada and most European countries held US in high esteem; US fares well above 50 in most countries including Latin

American countries. After the Iraq war
which occurred in 2003 under very
suspicious circumstances created by
the Bush administration, US standing
in the world plummeted to well under
50 in most countries. As the world
learned that it was an elaborate
scheme by the Bush administration to
go to war with Iraq, US standing on
the world stage had continued to
suffer and its rating continued to
plummet. Distrust of everything the US
government said was at an all-time
high. The world simply didn't want to
hear anything the US government had to
say. Cooperation was almost non-
existent because of the level of
distrust US allies had towards the
United States.

When Obama assumed the presidency, he
reset the world' view about US. He
visited Cairo, Egypt to re-assure the

world of US commitment to work towards peace and diplomacy instead of the previous administration approach which resulted almost exclusively in waging war against any country (overwhelmingly Muslim) the US didn't consider as ally. As such, the reversal in US foreign policy approach has contributed greatly to a gradual increase in US favorable standing on the world stage, except for a few Muslim countries (ironically) and Russia where US standing stays in the low ten's.

Trump's World View

Mr. Trump's position on various international issues has been wishy-washy at best. He is usually most inclined to "run with" someone else's opinion (about any issue) and debated it as if it were his views all along, until of course he changed those views again after watching a few news clips, reading a few commentaries and convinced himself he then had a complete understanding of the topic.

The behavior is nothing new to Donald Trump. In fact, he has managed to be "successful" using exactly that type of approach in business dealing and negotiation. The fact was most reflective in his presidential campaign website where it was quite obvious his understanding of foreign policy is very limited at best. But Donald Trump blindly trusts his instinct about most everything. He has good reason to; as pointed out earlier, he's been successful in the business world using such unorthodox approach. How hard can it possibly be to apply the same approach to governing, Mr. Trump must have reasoned.

During an interview accorded to Matt Lauer after clinching the nomination, Mr. Trump suggested that he listens to himself about foreign policy. After being ridiculed and confronted by the media, he revised his statement to suggest otherwise. But Mr. Trump believes his instinct completely, an attitude which could be great in some circumstances and a complete disaster in others.

For instance, after Obama toppled the Libyan leader Muammar Gaddafi, a political vacuum was created in the country and opened the country to many Islamic extremist groups which would later become responsible for the attacks on the US embassy in Benghazi.

Mr. Trump took to the airwaves to condemn the Obama administration to have removed Gaddafi. Ironically, a few months prior, Mr. Trump lambasted the Obama administration for being too slow in removing Gaddafi.

It is likely that Donald Trump may be completely unaware of his ignorance in foreign policy.
Or he may be so sure of his instinct, he might convince himself that nothing else matters in decision making.
Although one can appreciate Mr. Trump's modus of thinking, it is not at all re-assuring that the man whose words can literally change the world is very shortsighted in foreign policy. Instinct is good but can the country rely on what seems to be Donald Trump' strongest ability?

Although no one can deny that good
instinct might be an asset, it is
impossible to understand that Mr.
Trump could rely so much on his to
attend to the affairs of the country
on the international stage.

Be as it may, we can only hope that
his choice of Secretary of State may
help to bring some sanity into the
process of foreign policy and
international relations.
Then again, it may not matter. Mr.
Trump campaigned on the premise that
US comes first, an attitude which
might push his administration towards
crafting foreign policies overly
favorable to the country. Whether
other countries would go along, do the
same or retaliate is the key factor
which would determine the outcome of
Trump's policy. Already - as of this
writing - his administration announced

that Mr. Trump would re-negotiate NAFTA (North American Free Trade Agreement) and do away with TPP (Trans Pacific Partnership)

OBAMA GRADE

Despite the praise that Obama might have repaired US image abroad, the discussion on US foreign policy under his administration cannot be complete without taking a more in-depth look at his accomplishment on the international stage vis-à-vis several countries and more specifically in regards to events in those countries.

Foreign Policy is one aspect of the presidency which offers the most flexibility to any president. Contrary to domestic issues which require a great deal of negotiations and compromises with the Legislators in Washington, especially those of the opposing political party, the president is more or less free to enter into agreement with other countries, negotiate deals (arms, commerce) and even go to war without the restrictive hands of the opposition. As such, both success and failure of a president are fully under his control. How did Obama do in foreign policy? Mr. Obama got a C+ overall for his initiatives towards repairing US image abroad, re-establishing trust among US allies and opening the door for further alliances with countries which are still considered non-allies or enemies.

Although I previously outlined Obama's foreign policy, here I will take a more in-depth look at the most important events which took place across the globe and how the US under Obama has fared.

Egypt

Obama was the first president who had stepped into the Oval Office with a clear agenda to repair the country image abroad and most importantly to adopt a friendly approach in foreign policy instead of the bellicose posture the previous (and most) administration had used.

To that end, within just six months into his presidency, Obama made a historic trip to Cairo, Egypt on June 4, 2009 where he delivered a speech meant to outline the new approach in

US foreign policy towards the Arab World in general, the Middle East in particular. National Public Radio (NPR) described Obama foreign policy as follows: "Obama seeks new beginning with Muslim world".

By any analysis, Mr. Obama genuinely wanted to improve United States relations with the Arab community but there were several factors in play which were either ignored by his administration or simply overlooked. For starter, a single visit, a single speech by president Obama (or any US president) could not be defined as foreign policy, let alone foreign policy to shape relations between two countries or two regions. Second, the Arabs have always been very suspicious of the West activity in the region, for good reason (*the West had double crossed the Arab countries many times*

*in the past, detailed in my upcoming
book in regards to the conflicts
between Israel and the Palestine).*

So, Mr. Obama trip to the region and
the olive branch he extended were
considered positive steps but not
enough to move the needle for a
heartfelt welcome of the United States
by the Muslims in the region. After
all, the Arabs "saw that movie"
before. Third, Mr. Obama' speech was
considered a minor step in the grand
scheme of solving the problems which
have plagued the Arabs in general, the
Middle East in particular. Mere words
could not change that; the situation
in the Middle East could not possibly
be solved with the delivery of a
speech.

Mr. Obama got A for initiative; he
correctly identified a region in the

world which deserves a lot more attention than the United States has given; however, Mr. Obama failed to pursue a policy which could have changed the world in a major way. Most of the major acts of terror across the globe have roots in the Israeli-Palestine conflicts. Mr. Obama got an F for failing to follow-up in a game changing initiative.

Israel

The main crux of the problems in the
Middle East region was the making of
the West (UK, France, US); UN
Resolution 181 – (http://bit.ly/2hEBbYd) which
was drafted to divide The Palestine in
order to provide a country to the Jews
(Israel) has been violated by Israel
since its creation in 1948

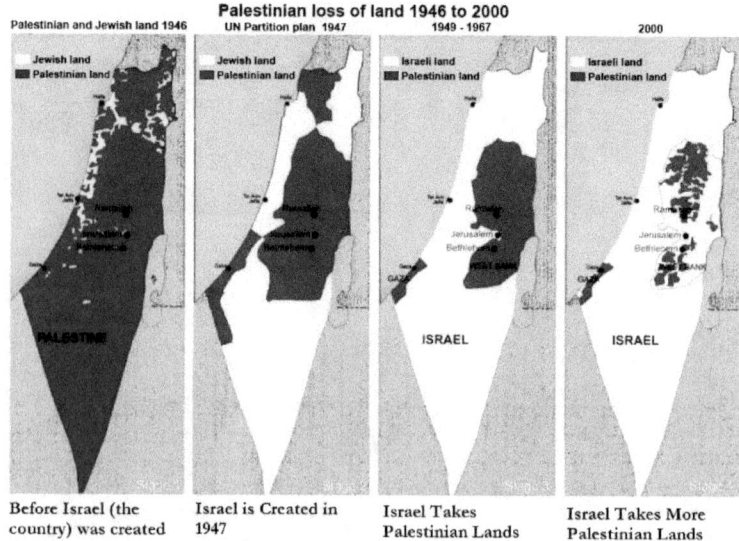

Palestinian loss of land 1946 to 2000

Palestinian and Jewish land 1946	UN Partition plan 1947	1949 - 1967	2000
Before Israel (the country) was created	Israel is Created in 1947	Israel Takes Palestinian Lands	Israel Takes More Palestinian Lands

but the West in general and US in
particular have at first turned a

blind eye to the conflicts between Israel and the Palestine and later sided with Israel - *provided security, intelligence, weapons, money to Israel* - with seemingly no intention to hold its ally responsible. So, no single speech from any US president could possibly change the predicament in the region unless the US government was to follow through with appropriate policies and actionable measures to remedy the situation, mainly to force Israel into compliance with the UN Resolution 181.

Obama quickly realized that US Middle East foreign policy (*in regards to Israel and the Palestine in particular*) is actually a domestic issue. - *To complicate matters, Mr. Obama is opposed by the Republican Party and most Republican Legislators in Washington in everything.* - Most

Americans favor Israel (*the mass for religious reason, the politicians for geopolitics reason*); as such, the Middle East region is just like a high voltage third rail to avoid by any president who would seek re-election. And Obama re-election bid began the day he was sworn into office for his first term. It was rather evident that the Obama administration was frustrated by the Israeli prime minister Netanyahu public stance on the issue of the conflicts in general, the settlements in particular. It was for the first time in a very longtime that a US president had kept a distance from Israel, considered by both Republican and Democrat administrations a strategic ally in the region. One would say that the relation between Israel and the United States during the Obama presidency was lukewarm at best, contentious mostly.

The relation between the two countries had gotten from "not good to bad" when prime minister Netanyahu sought re-election (http://nyti.ms/2i5tDPh) in March 2015. - *he promised to his hardcore supporters to continue the land grab policy and the constructions of more settlement projects, a statement that the Obama administration quickly denounced* - A short time later, the signing of the US Nuclear deal agreement with Iran contributed to exacerbate the situation and sour further the relation between the two countries. To make matters worse, at the invitation of then Republican Party House Speaker John Boehner, the Israel prime minister Benjamin Netanyahu came to US and delivered a speech to a joined session of Congress to rebuke Obama's deal with Iran. Granted that the Republicans were out of line and should have never invited a foreign entity to speak against the US president foreign policy, the prime minister crossed a very dangerous line in the relation with the United States. Israel would have paid a hefty political price had Obama continued a bit aggressively to pursue a change in US policy in the Middle East.

Although contrary to most presidents before him who had simply rubberstamped US position on Israel irrespective of its transgressions towards its neighbors in general, the Palestine in particular, Obama had tried several times to remedy the situation in the Middle East but like most US presidents serving a first term, Obama's priority to get re-elected was considered more important than trying to force Israel into compliance with the UN Resolution 181.

The prime minister of Israel Netanyahu who's been on the bloc longer than Obama accurately concluded that Obama didn't have the political will nor the courage to fight his Republican opponents for the implementation of UN Resolution 181(II). As such, the Obama administration followed a long list of US presidents who have failed to bring peace in the Middle East region. Like his predecessors, Obama publicly blamed the Palestinian fighters (HAMAS) for the situation in the region.

Mr. Obama got a C- for initiative and a failing grade for doing very little, probably much less than any president before him, to remedy the Israeli-Palestine conflicts. Instead of working towards a real solution, the Obama administration branded HAMAS a terrorist group. Suffice to say that

HAMAS is no more a terrorist group than THE PATRIOTS who fought for US independence were. The only rationale the US government has to brand HAMAS (the Palestinian Fighters) as a terrorist group is to de-legitimize their true purpose.

Israel Matters for Now

Mr. Trump's position on the Israeli-Palestine conflicts is unknown, undefined. He initially suggested that the two countries solve their own problems; under pressure by the Republican Party, Mr. Trump changed his position to re-iterate US support for Israel.

The world in general, the European countries in particular have changed their views on the conflicts in the Middle East, pushing the blame for the problems towards Israel's; as of this writing, it came through the wire that Israel has re-opened settlement constructions, betting that the Trump's administration would not object and would most likely veto any action taken by United Nations against Israel. President Trump signaled his intention to Israel by proposing to have the US embassy moved to Jerusalem from Tel-Aviv, a move which would most likely anger the Arab world.

Irrespective of that specific issue, it seems that the Trump administration has already set the stage to do away with most US allies.

Syria

It is impossible to discuss the human crisis in Syria without referring to George W. Bush; granted the Bush administration had no direct involvement with what has been going on in that country but his cavalier approach to starting war in the region had placed undue restrictions on his successor – *Obama* – and tied everyone's hands. Following the costly and ongoing war in Iraq which needed not be – *lies, deceptions fed to the American people were the basis for US to go to war with Iraq; the 9/11 attacks on US soil rendered the US civilians fearful of other attacks, more open to waging wars than to facing specters of other such attacks* – and after several years of bloodshed, loss of lives (*both American and Iraqi*) and a gargantuan war tab to be picked up by the taxpayers, - *in 2013, the cost of waging wars in Afghanistan and Iraq had reached four trillion dollars ($4T); according to a September 12, 2016 report by the publication "MilitaryTimes", the cost of the wars is now $5T* - Americans were not just tired of the wars, they were also reluctant to see the government engage in yet another war in the Middle East region.

Besides, the promises made by the Bush administration that the Iraq war would be a walk in the park and short lived weren't true; the US war machine would just go in, get rid of Saddam and get out. It was a fairy tale. Even as of this writing, US is involved in Iraq in some combat capacity. As such, Obama who had already condemned the ongoing war in Iraq and promised during his campaign bid for the White House in 2008 to end that war couldn't possibly invite the American people to foot up another bill for yet a new war. In addition, Obama has a natural aversion for wars; however, when rumors that the Syrian dictator Assad had used chemical gas against the rebels (*who have been fighting his regime*) and civilians, Obama was forced to take a harsh stance against the Syrian regime. He drew a red line in the sand in regards to the conflict between the Assad regime and the opposition; Mr. Obama publicly declared that US would take action if evidence was found that the dictator had used gas against his own people.

Whether to show defiance or to simply taunt the US president, the Syrian armed forces seemed to have made use of gas during confrontations with Assad's enemies. It was shortly thereafter verified that Assad's army had indeed used gas in the fight against the rebels. Obama found himself in a pickle, for it was humiliating for the US president not to act on his words and also excruciatingly difficult to go to war with Syria knowing darn well that the dictator had the full backing of the

Kremlin. Unless Obama was prepared to confront Russia in Syria, it was a call no US president would find easy to make.

The Red Line in the Sand

Obama was faced with the most difficult decision his administration had to make. Even to go after bin Laden could not have been nearly as difficult.

Obama's Red Line

With a parade of Republican officials (both current and former) on network televisions and over the airwaves and

an army of others publishing their
opinions on the internet, on social
media and in the major newspapers, all
of which had one main objective: to
push Obama to start a war with Syria,
Obama had to either make good on his
word or find an alternative quickly to
resolve the impasse.

The Republican machine, including past
administration officials namely former
vice president Dick Cheney and former
secretary of defense Donald Rumsfeld,
shifted gear to overdrive in their
continued assault of insults towards
Obama; they accused him of wavering
(which he did), spineless (which he
is), incompetent (I would not go that
far). Mr. Obama was labeled with every
derogatory term in the dictionary for
avoiding a war with Syria. Although it
was heart wrenching to watch the
disturbing images of children maimed,

disembodied and killed during the fights between the Assad' armed forces and the rebels, it was nevertheless a very difficult call to make by the US president to attempt to remove Assad or even to put an end to the fighting.

Syria backed by Russia

It was very easy for the Republicans (*or anyone for that matter*) to sit in the comfort of their homes and deliberate on Obama vis-à-vis his "non-action" on Syria. In addition to trying to avoid another war, Obama was in the unique position to assess the full effect of a war with Syria.

Contrary to the previous administration with an itch to take the country to war, Obama had always adopted a more deliberate approach; he took full inventory (*performed a full assessment*) of starting a war, maintaining peace and minimizing casualties on both sides. After all, though the objective was to simply remove Assad, there was the biggest obstacle Mr. Obama had to face, Russia.

The diplomatic relations between the Kremlin and Damascus were renewed in the course of the infighting between the Assad' army and the Rebels. Mr. Assad took a trip to the Kremlin – *a surprise and secret visit* – on October 21, 2015 to iron out whatever wrinkles between the two countries and secured military assistance from Russia. If Obama were to start a war with Syria, it was very certain the Kremlin would have been heavily involved militarily to defend or to help defending his ally Syria.

Irrespective of US war power, it was impossible to imagine that the outcome would have been swift like the war in Iraq; the casualties would have mounted quite quickly. Russia did warm up to Assad's visit; Mr. Putin was pleasantly surprised.

As a gesture to burying the hatchet and renewing relation with Assad, the Kremlin dispatched weapons to Syria to fight the rebels and personnel to help Assad strategize and to train the Syrian army. Although US logged complaints regarding the types of weapons the Assad army had used to fight the rebels, there was very little which could be done to force Assad out. And Obama knew that. Besides, US is also involved in the war, arming the rebels and providing them with intelligence and logistics.

In addition, there was a precedent. When the Kremlin offered to help US with the situation in Libya by withholding support (*military, logistics and intelligence*) from the Gaddafi regime, the Obama administration took advantage of Putin's generosity; he went much further than Russia would have wanted; in addition to removing weapons from Libya, US proceeded to remove Muammar

Gaddafi from power; he was later captured by the opposition and killed.

So, it was more or less certain that the Kremlin was not about to make the same mistake again. As such, the Obama administration did not have many options, for a war with Syria was an indirect war with Russia. Obama used the only available option, to negotiate removal of chemical weapons from Syria by Russia. Although most Obama's critics here at home lambasted him for letting Russia handle the chemical removal from Syria, however, from a diplomatic standpoint, that was a brilliant move by the Obama administration. Everyone got something, probably exactly what each party may have wanted in the first place a) Assad wanted to come clean and promised he would not use chemical weapons; he would not if they were no

longer available to use, giving US
(and the rest of the World) peace of
mind that no more gas would be used
against the civilians b) Mr. Putin was
pleased that Russia was responsible to
remove the weapons; although the
Kremlin "footed the bill" for the
removal, it was nevertheless pleased
to have those weapons in its
possession c) Obama was pleased that
Syria would no longer be able to use
deadly gas and was thus not obligated
to escalate the crisis to war level.
That was a close call! Despite much
criticism by the Republicans, such
arrangement was a much better
alternative than the spectre of
another war.

It is worth noting however that the
move by the Obama administration was
not to put an end to the conflicts
between Assad' regime and the Rebels.

Although the US had been supplying the rebels with weapons, logistics and intelligence, the Assad' regime had also received plenty of assistance from the Kremlin who has a vested interest to keep Assad in Syria in power. It is not at all clear whether any US president could end the civil war in Syria without heavy American casualties. To make matters worse, ISIS had been on the outskirts of Syria where they've blended with civilians to plan attacks and fight against the Iraqis and the US troops from the Iraqi border. The situation had also been exploited by Assad (and the Kremlin); air assault on the area was labeled by the Syrian regime and Russia as a fight against ISIS. The Assad' army used the opportunity to pummel the Rebels' positions, a claim made by the US government many times which fell on deaf ears.

Gas found – fabricated or planted

When it was revealed that the rumors regarding use of gas by the Syrian army on civilians were true,

it was great news here in the United States for Obama's critics as well as foes; they all reveled at the idea that the president was pushed to a corner which would force him to make

good on his word, mainly to go to war
with Syria. After all, he alone was
responsible to have drawn a line in
the sand. But Obama was not going to
let his critics dictate his move in
regards to the situation in Syria. His
aversion for "senseless or dumb" war
had been a guiding principle for his
administration whenever the specter of
war emerged. So, it was not at all
surprising to watch Obama looking for
alternative to going to war with Syria
despite the revelation that the line
he drew had been crossed. In
hindsight, it was a very smart move to
have avoided going to war over the
alleged use of gas by the Syrian army.

According to "France Diplomatie", a
French publication, the rumors of gas
used by the Syrian army on civilians
were bogus as reported on BBC.
According to the publication, the use

of chlorine gas by the Syrian army
helicopters would have caused tens of
thousands of victims in a matter of a
few hours, something which clearly
didn't happened. The publication
didn't refute the existence of the gas
but questioned whether it was ever
used by the Assad' regime as widely
and indiscriminately reported in the
US news media. "France Diplomatie"
questioned whether the very detection
of the gas on the battlefield could
even be attributed to Assad.

The differing opinion on the matter
clearly outlines the difficulty the
International agency – *United
Nations (UN)* - had to dispel rumors and
confirm any allegation. Similar
scenarios were present before the US
invasion of Iraq; elements in the
opposition to the Saddam regime
purposely fed the US government with

false information regarding the existence of WMD in Iraq in order to incentivize the expeditious removal of Saddam; the false information were used by the Bush administration to sell the Iraq war to the American people.

Obama didn't rush to action; his calculation was on point. It is my belief that Obama would have ordered an attack on Syria if he was convinced that the small amount of the gas detected was the direct action by the Syrian army on the civilians. Instead, he opted for the removal of the gas from Syria. Needless to speculate that the warmongers in Washington were not pleased with the solution! Although Obama had not ended the atrocities committed by the Assad' regime on the civilians, he averted another war.

History will nevertheless judge him
harshly for "doing nothing" to stop
the atrocities but the situation in
Syria was not black and white either.
To complicate matters, it was believed
that the very elements (ISIS and ISIS
sympathizers) US was fighting in the
region (Iraq, Libya, Yemen and
elsewhere) would take hold of power in
Syria should Assad be removed, hardly
a desired alternative.

Obama got a "C-" in regards to the
situation in Syria; although to go to
war to remove Assad seemed to be the
most popular option among the
Republicans in Washington, Obama knew
better. The situation in Iraq was
still not the outcome anyone expected
after the removal of Saddam; in
addition to hundreds of thousands of
Iraqis killed, over a million
displaced, Iraq was still not any

better than when Saddam Hussein was in control. One might even argue that it is now worse. Before the US Invasion of Iraq in 2003 by the Bush administration, Saddam was able to keep all the various factions in check, and there was no ISIS. So, Obama was right not to have taken the bait to start a war with Syria. However, he did not create a scenario to use or work with in order to address the crisis either. The world watched in disbelief the mounting civilian casualties while the superpowers (US, UK, Germany, France, Russia, Spain, China) had done little to nothing.

Unfortunately, the Obama administration believed the president was doing something; he tasked the Pentagon (http://bit.ly/2igGuxt) to create a framework which would provide the rebels some leverage over the Assad' army. Although I am no expert in the matter, it seems illogical that any plan without Russia participation, no matter how well conceived, would succeed. 1) there was the Russia factor; Assad had the full backing of the Kremlin 2) up to this point, there was not a single entity which could be entrusted the governing of the country should Assad be removed 3) ISIS was well represented in the various factions vying for power in Syria.

There were however three course changing options, *one more desirable than the other two*, Obama could have explored, either one of which if adopted early on would have by now brought the desired outcome.

1.- **Get Rid of Assad Forcefully**: the first one would be to train a team of "mercenaries" or "special forces" to assassinate Assad. – *I do cringe over the idea of assassination but the US government is no stranger to making use of the practice* - Great! Assad would be killed, captured or fled to Russia, then what? Well, the fall of Assad would create a void which would need to be filled rather quickly. This option does not however guarantee a peaceful transition in Syria. As it stands today, there are many factions which vie for power. In addition to the possibility that the military would have seized power and made the situation worse, there was also the likelihood that Mr. Putin might have decided to occupy Syria. Did either of those two scenarios seem better than the Assad regime in power? It was a decision Obama would have to make with the help of his advisors.

2.- **Get Rid of Assad with kindness:**
the second option which is the most
desirable one was to negotiate –
notice I didn't say order, bully, ask,
threaten – Assad' departure from Syria
with Assad. This is the most difficult
option but also the most rewarding
with the least casualties, if any.
This option would require a lot of
incentives, a lot of convincing, a lot
of Assad' participation in negotiation
and a lot of Russia's help but it
would be worthwhile as well. This
option would provide enough time to
plan for an interim government, to
draft a constitution or amended one
(if necessary) and to organize
election and implement the process but
most importantly to rein in the armed
forces. This option would also require
the United States government to
relinquish control to Russia to make
it happen. This option requires a lot

of patience, a lot of back and forth discussions and a willingness to be generous towards Assad's demands (Money, Security, etc.) The objective would not be immediate rewards, so it would be okay for Russia to be in control of the process; such arrangement would warrant a much less chaotic transition and provide all parties a possibility to participate in the process of government.

3.- **Get Rid of Assad slowly with kindness:** the third option which may not be liked by all parties is to keep Assad in power and task him to announce upcoming election in five years. Despite all, Assad is the best person to introduce his impending departure and prepare the Syrians to participate in free election in the near future. This option seems to be the best to transition the Armed

Forces into accepting an elected
president. Contrary to option 2 which
tries to get rid of Assad quickly,
this option would give him time to
begin accepting the idea of a civilian
life, even to try it out by taking
some vacation during the five- years
period. This option would also require
patience, a lot of incentives and a
willingness to show him a lavishing
lifestyle without the worries (of
assassination, trial for war crimes,
etc). With the help of his wife who is
already very familiar with and has
embraced the western lifestyle, it may
not be as difficult as it sounds.
Besides, despite having set a maximum
of five years to perform the
transition, Mr. Assad would have the
flexibility to leave before the
expiration of his time in Syria. This
option would also prevent Assad from
being a candidate in the upcoming

election (even if he were allowed to stay in the country; preferably not), thus preventing fraud or chaos during the election. Such arrangement would give all parties ample time to prepare, Assad to make plan to leave Syria and settle somewhere for the rest of his civilian life, the other political parties to begin the process of choosing their next president.

Thus far, the Obama administration has relied on too many variables a) the framework by the Pentagon to free Syria of the Assad regime b) the arming of the Rebels c) the negotiating of the cease fire d) the negotiating with Russia for Assad' departure.
All of which shows a high level of indecisiveness on the part of Obama regarding the Syrian crisis.

Trump Partners with Putin

Could the Trump administration solve
the Syrian crisis problem? Trump seems
to hint at a joint effort between the
US and Russia in order to "eviscerate"
ISIS. Mr. Trump has promoted the idea
for a very longtime now; he seems very
convinced that Russia's participation
in a campaign against ISIS will be
successful.

Although impossible to know at this
point whether such alliance would
work, it will however open the
opportunity for Russia (and Syria) to
completely eliminate the Rebels as
well, thus far a thorn in Assad' eye.

Such collaboration would also make it
near impossible for US to contemplate
the idea of ending the Assad regime.

Ghost of Iraq war

At the time the Republicans were
lining up to drum up the beat of war,
70% of the US population did not
approve of the United States going to
war with Syria. That sentiment was a
major departure from an electorate who
have always supported the idea for the
government to take the war to the
enemy instead of fighting it out here
on the homeland. But the warmongers
weren't deterred; as far as they were
concerned, the president should do
what's best for the American people –
*like George W. Bush did when he took
the country to war in Iraq under false
pretext* – even if the people disagree.
Fortunately, despite the hatred
expressed by most Republicans towards
Obama, he was a president who seemed
to have more respect for the will of

the people; much, much less can be said about past Republican presidents.

It is quite refreshing that every now and then a president would actually do what We The People want. When it came to engaging in wars, one could rest assured that Obama would not make use of the servicemen and women on a whim. It was rather ironic that so many armed services personnel (servicemen and women) did not revere Obama who had always valued their lives and agonized over putting them in arms way to the service of the country. It seemed that the ghost of the Iraq war did not scare off the servicemen and women.

Iraq / Afghanistan

In his bid for the presidency in 2008, then candidate Barack Obama made it clear that he was against the war in Iraq; he never criticized nor condemned the Bush administration to have engaged in war in Afghanistan. After all, it was in Afghanistan that the training of the operatives which carried out the 9/11 attacks on US took place. So, Obama understood that the American president had to respond if it's only to let US enemies know that any terrorist action on America and American interests would not go unpunished. It is safe to conclude that Obama would have also punished the Taliban in Afghanistan had the attacks on US soil happened during his presidency.

However, the Iraq war could have been
avoided.

Even if Saddam's regime had Weapons of
Mass Destructions (WMD) as the Bush
administration propagandized in order
to secure the approval of the American
people, the International Atomic
Energy Agency (IAEA – https://www.iaea.org/)
team was on the ground in Iraq
conducting searches for said weapon
when the Bush administration ordered
its personnel out or suffered whatever

consequences would ensue of a US air attacks on Iraq.

Barack Obama, in a speech delivered on October 2002, a few months prior to the Iraq war in March 2003, said "... *I stand before you as someone who is not opposed to war in all circumstances... I don't oppose all wars... What I am opposed to is a dumb war... Now let me be clear — I suffer no illusions about Saddam Hussein. He is a brutal man. A ruthless man. A man who butchers his own people to secure his own power... But I also know that Saddam poses no imminent and direct threat to the United States or to his neighbors... I know that even a successful war against Iraq will require a U.S. occupation of undetermined length, at undetermined cost, with undetermined consequences. I know that an invasion of Iraq without a clear rationale and without strong international support will only fan the flames of the Middle East, and encourage the worst, rather than best, impulses of the Arab world, and strengthen the recruitment arm of al-Qaida. I am not opposed to all wars. I'm opposed to dumb wars."*

In hindsight, it seems that Barack Obama was a prophet. If legislators then had the gut, the wherewithal and the wisdom to legislate, billions of dollars spent in the war in Iraq could have been saved, thousands of lives lost and millions of others affected by a senseless war could have been avoided. But most importantly, the world would probably not have had to fight ISIS, an enemy which is nowhere and everywhere, an enemy which cannot be defeated by a strong army or the most sophisticated weapons, an enemy which can and have morphed at will.

ISIS is the immediate by-product of the disbanding of the Iraqi army by the US government.

Having inherited the war he tried to warn us about, Mr. Obama had to work towards gradually putting an end to both the war in Iraq as well as the one in Afghanistan, and to reduce the number of servicemen and women stationed in those "hot spots". But the plan to withdraw US military presence from both Iraq and Afghanistan was as delicate as the plan to go to war should have been; Iraq was no longer ruled by Saddam who managed to keep the various factions in the country together; Afghanistan was no longer run by the Taliban who warranted a semblance of normal life to the residents. Both countries were in complete state of chaos, and despite the US military presence and

quite possibly because of it, daily
suicide explosions were stark
reminders that *to win a war could no
longer be defined as to defeat an
army*.

In Iraq, the absence of the Saddam
regime and the dismantling of his army
*- well trained officers and soldiers
with no prospect of a job is a deadly
enemy to fight against under the best
of circumstances* - gave rise to ISIS.

Although Republican politicians want
to attribute the rise of ISIS to
Obama's policy in Iraq, it was the

Bush administration which created the deadliest terrorist group. When the Saddam's army was completely disbanded, its officers were sent off to fend off for themselves financially.

It doesn't take a genius to figure out that those highly trained soldiers, officers, captains and generals, now unemployed would not simply walk away and sit on their hands. Ironically, that's exactly what was going to happen according to the genius Paul Bremer (*head of the Coalition Provisional Authority*) appointed by the Bush administration to run Iraq as its interim Administrator; Saddam's disbanded officers had no choice, the genius reasoned. To the genius' surprise, those highly trained former Saddam's armed forces soldiers disappeared for a while and re-

organized into what would become the
most lethal terrorist group in the
world. With an army structure, combat
training and soldiers' endurance, the
group introduced itself to the world
under the banner of Islamic State of
Iraq and the Levant (ISIL) or Islamic
State in Iraq and Syria (ISIS).

Overnight, ISIS had become notorious
for its egregious atrocities and its
blatant disregard for human lives;
even Al-Qaeda leaders had condemned
some of the atrocities committed by

ISIS' members. Today, ISIS represents a nightmare for the world leaders.

Obama got a "C" for his handling of the troops' reduction in Iraq and Afghanistan. While the reduction in combat troops was necessary to end the wars and wind down the military occupations of those two countries, most Republicans were very critical of Obama' decision to reduce the armed service personnel from both Iraq and Afghanistan. Republicans have always considered the presence of US troops anywhere in the world as a permanent affair; they seem to be right. As of date, US has troops stationed almost everywhere in the world; there are US military bases in all seven continents. For instance, in Japan alone, US has 84 military bases; in Germany, one can find US military bases in more than 30 locations.

Despite Obama's best effort to reduce the size of the troops in Iraq and Afghanistan, it proved near impossible to simply close those US military bases. The psychological comfort we Americans have experienced because of US troops' presence in every corner of the world is no comfort at all, especially in regards to terrorist threats such as those posed by groups like ISIS (or Al-Qaeda). It is a loosely organized terror group which extends flexibility to everyone and anyone who wants to spread terror in the name of ISIS. As such, it is extremely difficult (if not impossible) to prevent terror from happening.

But despite the terror caused by the ISIS group throughout the world, Obama had made it top priority to prevent any tragedy the group would have inflicted on America homeland. The Obama administration had dedicated tremendous amount of resources to combat ISIS here at home and abroad. Just a few months away from the end of his presidency, the president's effort to keep the country shielded from major terror attacks seem to be paying off.

Trump to end ISIS

It is worth noting that Trump is more concerned about ISIS in the area than in Iraq as a country. If one were to judge by his past comments about US involvement everywhere, the Trump's administration would not concern itself of any internal issue in any country.

Iran

Iran has had a very complicated relation with the United States in the past six to seven decades.

US Embassy in Iran before the Iranian Revolution in 1979

For over two decades (*the early 1950's to the early 1970's*), the relation between the two countries was very friendly.

Iran was ruled at the time by Mohammad Reza Shah Pahlavi - *commonly referred*  *to as the Shah of Iran or simply the Shah* - from September 1941 till his overthrow during the Iranian revolution in February 1979.

The Iranian Revolution brought with it a slew of problems for the West in general, the United States in particular. Supreme Leader Ayatollah Khomeini who  made no secret of his disapproval for the relation the Shah had with the United

To complicate matters, when the US government reluctantly offered exile to the Shah who was believed to be dying of cancer, a group of Iranian students, belonging to the Muslim Student Followers of the Imam's Line, who supported the Iranian Revolution, stormed the U.S. Embassy in Tehran on November 4, 1979 and took 60 occupants hostage.

The Iranians believed that the US government (then a.k.a. president Jimmy Carter administration) fabricated a story in regards to the Shah's health. Iran demanded his return to stand trial for crimes against Iranian citizens committed through SAVAK, the Shah' secret police. Iranians interpreted the

decision by the Carter administration
to grant him asylum and not comply
with their demands as sign of the
American government complicity in
those atrocities. Khomeini's followers
retaliated and vowed not to give in
until their demands were met.

Then US president Jimmy Carter would
ultimately pay the political price (*of
losing his re-election bid to Ronald
Reagan*) for the hostage crisis which
lasted over a year (*444 days, November
4, 1979, to January 20, 1981*).

The United States government was
obviously not happy with the Ayatollah
but no US president in the right frame
of mind would want to engage in a war
with Iran under "frivolous"
circumstances such as the hostage
crisis; any such engagement could

destabilize the region and most likely would drag Israel into the quagmire.

After a failed attempt to rescue the hostages left eight US servicemen dead and two aircraft destroyed, the US government capitulated and asked the Shah to leave the United States; he would spend the rest of his days in Egypt where he is believed to have died of complications from the cancer illness on July 27, 1980.

The Shah' passing did not however put an end to the standoff at the US embassy in Iran but something totally unrelated happened which would eventually change the dynamic of the hostage crisis. Iraqi leader Saddam Hussein, sensing an opportunity during the chaotic moments of the Iranian Revolution, launched an attack by land

and by air against Iran on September 22, 1980. The assault was not meant to free the hostages but complicated matter for the new Iranian leader who had just begun to get a handle on governing; the Ayatollah was forced to seek a resolution for the Embassy crisis; besides, the reason for the hostage situation was gone with the death of the Shah. With Algeria acting as a mediator, Iran negotiated the release of the hostages to United States' custody the day after the signing of the Algiers Accords. (http://bit.ly/2i5zTGC) - The release of the hostages felt more like good riddance to the Carter administration by the Iranians - *in fact, it was; the Iranians blamed the Carter administration for supporting the Shah during his ruling and providing him exile after fleeing the country* - and a welcome party for the new president;

the hostages were released mere
minutes after Ronald Reagan was sworn
into office.

The release of the hostages was
however a completely separate event
from the war Iraq had just started
against its neighbor Iran a few months
ago. Although Saddam had made some
progress in the early days of the war,
by 1982 there was a stalemate. The
Reagan administration seized the
golden opportunity (the stalemate in
the war) to use Iraq as a proxy in
order to retaliate against the
Ayatollah, since the Algiers Accords
prevented the United States from
interfering in Iran's affairs. Through
Dick Cheney and Donald Rumsfeld
(http://bit.ly/2i7Jwq0) as envoys to the Iraqi
regime, the Reagan administration
courted Saddam and began to provide
weapons, logistics and intelligence to

Iraq to aid with the war against its neighbor. In an effort to help its new found ally Iraq speed up the capitulation of Iran, the US government supplied chemical weapons to Saddam and encouraged him to make use of such – *there lies the mystery of the George W. Bush administration accusing Saddam of having WMD; his administration knew the US government (Ronald Reagan administration via CIA) supplied WMD to Iraq to use in the war against Iran but what the Bush' administration failed to realize was that the Saddam regime may have made use of it all. The Bush war strategists wrongly concluded that Saddam had the knowledge to culture the gas and built his own weapons. Because the regime did not anticipate a sudden stop of supplies, the war was still ongoing, Iraq was not in a position to build chemical delivery*

type of weapons – However, as the war
prolonged, the US without warning
stopped providing both weapons and
logistics to the Saddam regime
although the CIA continued for a while
to provide intelligence. The war
between the two countries lasted well
over six years until a peace deal was
brokered by UN in August 1988.

The end of the war between Iraq and
Iran did not do anything to bring the
two countries (US and Iran) back to
the friendly relation they once had.
If anything, the war gave the
Ayatollah and its supporters more
ammunition against the US government;
the Iranian leaders became aware that
the United States provided weapons,
intelligence and logistical support to
the Iraqis during the war and
correctly guessed that US must have
supplied the gas Saddam's army used on

the Iranian civilians. – *Has it not phased you that the US government, at its discretion, can make use of gas in wars but conveniently condemn its use by others?* - Over the next few decades, the tension between the United States and Iran exacerbated, an incentive for the Ayatollah to explore the possibility to build sophisticated weapons and long range missiles. The Iranian government, with assistance from Russia, had successfully built underground facilities for research and manufacture of sophisticated weapons of war; those facilities were built to sustain heavy bombardment in case of war, thus making it near impossible for US to destroy their weapon manufacture capability. In addition, Iran possess both naval and air force capability which can offer serious challenge to the US counterparts. As such, from Ronald

Reagan era to today, US presidents
have been careful to avoid direct
confrontation with Iran. A war with
Iran would most likely have
unpredictable geopolitical impact in
the region. In addition to having full
support from Russia, to complicate
matters further, the Iranian
government has made construction
and/or acquisition of nuclear weapons
and/or capability a priority.

Although materials to achieve nuclear

weapons
production are
not easy to
come by, and
acquisition of
raw materials would require long
periods of enrichment (*nine months+ or
longer depending on the desired
amount*) in addition to the time needed
for transportation, preparation and

storage, the US government has always been leery of a nuclear Iran. So, when Obama was just a candidate vying for the Oval Office in 2008, he commented that as president he would be willing to meet with US enemy in general, Iran in particular. His opponent John McCain, the Republican nominee, jumped on the opportunity to lambast Obama of the "ridiculous" idea to meet with Iran.

Although Obama walked back from the idea (*of meeting with the Iranian leader*) during the 2008 campaign, once in office, he worked with leaders of other countries (Russia, UK, France, China, Germany) to draft a nuclear deal agreement with Iran in which Iran would only pursue nuclear research and development for peaceful use only (i.e. electricity).

Obama gets A for not only securing the agreement but also for setting policy of unannounced visits by the International Atomic Energy Agency (IAEA) into Iran. In exchange, the Obama administration agreed to unfreeze (*from US and International financial institutions*) money owned by Iranian government and companies and to pay Iran for the weapon deal agreement with the Reagan administration (later referred to as the Iran contra affair – (http://bit.ly/2hEPcoz))

Despite much criticism by the Republican Party leaders, the Iran Nuclear deal agreement was a great achievement by Obama to rid the world of at least one country with ambition to acquire and/or manufacture nuclear weapons. Most Republicans who opposed the agreement cited the likelihood

that Iran will not abide by the
agreement. Be as it may, the agreement
not only guarantees surprise visits
into Iran but also provides the
latitude of visits anywhere in the
country without having to cooperate
with the Iranian government schedule
or activity.

In addition, the agreement provides US
and the other participant countries to
re-impose financial sanctions on Iran
should its government violate any
aspect of the agreement.
While it is probably true there is a
likelihood that Iran might attempt to
circumvent the agreement, the
financial pressure which would be put
on the country may be enough for the
Iranians to force its government into
compliance.
Irrespective of what ensues in the
future, it is undeniable that such

deal is a positive step towards controlling the proliferation of nuclear weapons.

Trump's Dilemma on Iran

For reason which is yet to meet any logical rationale, Mr. Trump has floated the idea that, as president, he would void the Nuclear Deal agreement with Iran by the six world powers, (P5+1: the United States, the United Kingdom, Russia, France, and China—plus Germany) a move which would certainly force the World Superpowers to bypass US in future negotiations which might have a worldwide.

Such attitude of the Trump's administration may have the opposite effect to Making America Great Again.

It's uncertain whether Trump believes America could be great alone. The world would no longer wait for US to lead, and its participation in the world affairs may become optional. While it's still unclear whether Mr. Trump is operating out of the GOP playbook, – to undo everything Obama – that particular agreement (with Iran) could become the catalyst which might redefine geopolitics balance in the world. It is not immediately possible to see any benefit of doing so, but the fallout could be catastrophic.

On the one hand, there is Russia which has been aggressively setting its footprints everywhere even in areas which were once considered US territories (or the NATO): the middle East, Africa and East Asia. On the other hand, there is China which has been hinting at picking up the leadership role should US (under the Trump administration) become a nationalist country.

Either or both scenarios would put US at a serious disadvantage on the world stage post Trump's presidency. Whichever country assumes the leadership role would not simply hand it back to US after Trump exits (or push out of) the Oval Office.

Cuba

The embargo on Cuba was put in place at a time when the world was starkly divided between allies and enemies during the Cold War (http://bit.ly/2fOVJKh).

It was never because the small island was ruled by a dictator. In fact, four months after leading a successful revolution in Cuba in 1959, Fidel Castro (the dictator) came to the

United States on an 11-day visit at
the invitation of the American Society
of Newspaper Editors. Mr. Castro
placed a wreath on George Washington's
monument, toured the Bronx Zoo and ate
hot dogs and hamburgers at the Yankee
Stadium.

For the most part, the visit went well
until his
speech at the
Council on
Foreign
Relations in
New York
during which

Mr. Castro underlined that he would
not "beg" the United States for
economic assistance. – *Can any logical
individual see anything wrong with the
president of another country making
such statement? Of course not but
those boys in Washington demand that*

*leaders of all small nations BEG for
assistance or else* - That didn't sit
well with the US government. US-Cuba
relation had deteriorated rapidly from
that point onward.

After many attempts by the CIA to
assassinate the Cuban leader failed,
the agency came up with the ultimate
plan to overthrow the regime.
Two years following Mr. Castro's visit
to the United States, the Central
Intelligence Agency (CIA) put in
motion a plan, Bay of Pigs operation
(http://bit.ly/2f0WR0t) a military invasion of
Cuba undertaken by the CIA-sponsored
paramilitary group Brigade 2506 on
April 17, 1961 to oust Castro.
Needless to point out that the attempt
to overthrow the Castro regime failed
and the mission was a complete fiasco.

Notice that up to this point Mr.
Castro did nothing wrong to the United
States government or the American
people; he merely stated his position
in regards to economic assistance for
his country which incidentally he had
every right to do.

As it has always been with everything
Washington does in the name of the
American People, there was no
justification to attempt to overthrow
Fidel Castro. It is perhaps worth
repeating here that the operation – *to
oust Mr. Castro* – was a complete
disaster, thus increasing the
political tensions between the two
countries. As it is expected in any
rancor, both sides would employ and
use tactics to hurt the opponent. So
it went, Cuba nationalized close to
one billion dollar of US Assets in the
island and US placed an embargo on

Cuba. That was in essence the issue at the heart of US-Cuba unfriendly relations.

But the US government had lied to the American people for well over 50 years and accused the Castro regime of sponsoring terrorism – *although there is never a single shred of evidence Cuba is involved in any act of terrorism* - and violating human rights. The propaganda – *with the complicity of the US media of course, always ready to lend a hand to the government* – has been so ingrained in the American consciousness that even past presidents (*latest was Bill Clinton in 1999*) had tightened sanctions against the impoverished island based on erroneous, exaggerated and fabricated accusations; US government must have its way with Cuba at all cost.

Most unfortunately as well, the body
of government which is supposed to
represent the American people (Houses
of Representatives in Washington) went
along and passed several measures to
tighten and keep in place the embargo
against Cuba and to continue to
isolate the island.

Ironically, despite the economic
pressure, Mr. Castro had continued to
run Cuba as best as any leader could
under such conditions; dictatorship
aside, Castro has done an excellent
job with the healthcare system in the
country, way better job than the
United States whose healthcare system
is twenty times as expensive.

According to a 2014 article in
Politifact citing Senator Tom Harkin,
Cuba has lower child mortality and
longer life expectancy than the United
States. As it stands today, Cuba has
more doctors than any country in the
world; for over five decades, the
Cuban government has always been the
first to send medical assistance to
any part of the world where disasters
(natural and man-made) strike. There
is even a FREE medical school program
(http://bit.ly/2dSLvOc) offered in the island

to anyone who has no objection living in Cuba (*all expenses paid by the Cuban government; no kidding!*) for the duration of the studies (5 to 6 years).

The embargo on Cuba had served only two purposes, both of which are despicable acts towards a neighbor nation which did not initiate any aggression or represent any threat 1) to establish that US government has no qualm stomping on small countries which do not go along with what it wants and 2) to punish the people of said countries financially.

So, it was rather embarrassing and quite shameful to hear any argument, especially from US Senator of Florida Marco Rubio, against the lifting of the embargo. Insanity, it's said, is doing the same thing over and over and over and expecting a different outcome. After 50 years of doing the same thing, it should have been obvious to the "smart" boys in Washington - *Presidents and Legislators* - that 1) the embargo did not and cannot work 2) the US government was wrong to place the embargo on Cuba in the first place.

Mr. Obama got an A for seeing the lifting of the embargo through. The American people, the nation as a whole should praise President Obama to have broken the cycle of insanity deeply ingrained in Washington's consciousness vis-à-vis Cuba. The lifting of the embargo was not checkmate for Mr. Obama or a victory for Mr. Castro; it is a relief for the people of Cuba, the primary victims of the embargo. That should be welcome news to everyone, especially Senator

Marco Rubio whose family roots originate from the island.

President Obama was the first president in a very longtime who has made use of back channel communication and negotiation with the intention to re-establish full relations (diplomatic and commercial) with the targeted country. As such, away from prying eyes and ears, the Obama administration enlisted the help of our neighbor Canada to initiate conversation with the leader of Cuba, Raoul Castro - *brother of Fidel Castro, the Revolutionary who overthrew his predecessor Fulgencio Batista* - who was at the time the ruler of the impoverished island. The news that such negotiation occurred came out with the final outcome that Obama proposed 1) to lift the trade embargo on Cuba 2) to open commercial

relation with the island 3) to
establish diplomatic relations with
its government. The Republican
legislators as expected vowed to block
any policy that would help the lifting
of the embargo; besides, they believed
it's bad for the United States. After
all, it was an initiative by Obama.
How could any move by Obama be good
for the United States! Unbelievable!

Barack Obama & Raoul Castro during his visit in Cuba

To jumpstart the process, in March
2016, the president and his family

traveled to Cuba, met with its leader Raoul Castro, visited historic sites and sat down with business entrepreneurs and dissidents of the regime. That was the first visit of a sitting US president in 90 years.

Although the lifting of the embargo and the re-establishing of relations between the two countries were not magical wands to wish Cuba problems away, they were important steps to help solving (or beginning to) economic problems and fixing social ones. Besides, the embargo on Cuba, as previously stated, was one of the most ridiculous and unwarranted actions the US government took in regards to foreign relation. In reality, it was the US government' action – *the attempt to overthrow Castro in the "Bay of Pigs" plot because he refused to "beg" US for economic assistance* -

which pushed Cuba to make alliance
with the Soviet Union (the Union of
Soviet Socialist Republics or
U.S.S.R.). Obama was absolutely right
to have put an end to the US
government insanity.

Trump on Cuba

It is highly unlikely that Mr. Trump
would alter the changes Obama made in
regards to Cuba; if anything, the
lifting of the embargo was welcome
news for Donald Trump. According to
reports, Mr. Trump has been conducting
business in Cuba through the embargo
period despite specific US laws
prohibiting all US companies from
engaging in commercial activities in
and with Cuba. In other words, Mr.
Trump has been in violation of the US
trade embargo on. It's difficult to

know whether he approved of the
embargo. However, during the general
elections, to align with the GOP view
on the issue, – mainly to disagree
with everything Obama – Mr. Trump
threatened to reverse diplomatic
relations with Cuba but a year prior,
as reported on the Sept 8, 2015 issue
of Wall Street Journal, Mr. Trump said
that said "he supported the Obama
administration's opening with Cuba."
Regardless, it's not expected his
administration would change much of
the lifting of the embargo. It seems
more likely he would work to expand
commercial relations between the two
countries, a move which would benefit
his personal business.
According to report, Mr. Trump owns
vineyards in Cuba. There is however
the other side of the coin to
consider, the lifting of the embargo
would put Mr. Trump's business in

direct competition with several other businesses in which scenario he might lose the advantage he now has. It's worth repeating that Mr. Trump's business has been operating in violation of the trade embargo. It would be interesting to see whether a reversal of Obama's policy towards Cuba by the Trump's administration would also trigger a prosecution of his own company for operating in violation of the embargo.

Ukraine

Ukraine is a country in Eastern Europe which is bordered in the East and Northeast by Russia, in the Northwest by Belarus, in the West by Poland, Slovakia and Hungary, in the Southwest by Romania and Moldova and in the South and Southeast by the Black Sea and Sea of Azov.

In addition to sharing borders with Russia in two separate locations,

Ukraine used to be one of the countries in the Soviet Republic (U.S.S.R.) until 1991 when Ukraine acquired its independence as a result of the Republic dissolution at the end of the Cold War.

So, it is not difficult to understand Russia's continued interest in Ukraine. After its independence, the two countries initially enjoyed a very friendly relation for a while; Ukraine even had a limited military partnership with the Russian Federation but because of its neutral position (*i.e. not belonging to one side – Russia or the other – the West: US, UK, Germany, etc.*) it also formed partnership with the North Atlantic Treaty Organization (NATO - http://www.nato.int/). However, when former pro-Russia President Viktor Yanukovych rejected the idea for

Ukraine to join NATO as a member, it was a decision which created a crisis commonly referred to in the news as the Ukraine Crisis.

Here is in a nutshell what the crisis was all about.

The crisis in Ukraine started on November 21, 2013 shortly after then President Viktor Yanukovych made an announcement to abandon an agreement to strengthen ties with the European Union but to instead seek closer cooperation with Moscow. Ukrainians were not happy with Yanukovych's decision. Protesters took to the streets.

Over the next few weeks, occasional clashes with police and demands made by the protesters escalated to violence; several arrests were made. On January 22, 2014, three protesters

died during a confrontation with the
police and on February 18, 2014, 26

people died
and hundreds
of others
injured. That
was the
beginning of a
crisis which would continue to
increase the tension between the
government and the protesters.

On February 20, 2014, merely hours

after a truce
between the
government
and the
protesters,

violence erupted again and took a turn
for the worst; government snipers on
rooftops who were supposed to monitor
the situation and used tear gas to
disperse the crowd gunned down well

over 80 protesters; that was the
tipping point for the violence to
reach the boiling stage, a mass
protest which could no longer be
controlled or restrained. The crisis
deteriorated rapidly from protesters
who wanted their voices heard to an
uprising against the government,
mainly then president Viktor
Yanukovych. Protesters' demand
upgraded to asking for the resignation
of the president.

In order to avoid further bloodshed
and ward off a military intervention
by the West (read United States),
Vladimir Putin, then Russia'
president, ordered its troops into
Ukraine. By any analysis, Mr. Putin
had very good and compelling reasons
to be concerned about the crisis in
Ukraine and involved in crafting a
peaceful resolution among the

competing parties; after all, Ukraine is located in Russia's backyard. But despite the presence of Russian army, the popular uprising against a government killing its own people was not about to let up. Therefore, then Ukraine president Viktor Yanukovych was forced to resign and fled to Moscow. The US government saw Yanukovych's departure as a victory for Ukraine and an opportunity for the West. In order to warrant US military presence in the country, the Obama administration, via Secretary of State John Kerry quickly promised one billion (with a B) dollar loan guarantees to Ukraine.

The departure of Viktor Yanukovych did not however end the crisis; historians would say that the crisis got worse. Ukrainians' opinions were split over what needed to be done; although most (citizens) of the country preferred to stay autonomous, the Crimean Peninsula - *or Crimea as it is commonly referred to* - wanted annexation with Russia. In a situation such as the crisis, Ukraine's constitution warranted for a referendum to be held to provide the people (of Crimea) the opportunity to decide the course of action through the referendum. Accordingly, on Sunday, March 16, 2014, a referendum was held in Crimea. The people of Crimea overwhelmingly (96%) voted to annex with Russia.

As far as Ukraine was concerned, the crisis was over. The people of Crimea had spoken; so, Crimea was now part of Russia but the Obama administration was not happy. There is usually a certain level of hypocrisy in the part of the US government when it comes to democracy; it seems that democracy takes whatever definition the US government wants it to be. Out of two million (2,000,000) Crimean, 1.9 million voted to rejoin Russia but for reason that only Washington could understand or explain, 96% of the residents of Crimea stated unequivocally their desire to have Crimea rejoined Russia was not enough proof that the People of Crimea wanted annexation with Russia. – *In the United States, it's impossible to get 75% of those eligible to vote to go to the polls on election day* - So, to show dissatisfaction with the will of the people of Crimea, the Obama administration imposed sanctions on a short list of pro-Russia Ukrainian officials. Have you ever asked yourself the simple question: what exactly does the US government believe in? What does it want? Democracy or Control? The Crimea referendum was a perfect example to figure out the US government agenda; here is a situation where 96% of the people wanted something but the US government was against it. Unbelievable!

Contrary to the US government propaganda, Crimean voters were happy and expressed their contentment to rejoin Russia. Thousands of voters took to the streets to express joy and happiness. Voter Manita Meshchina said "Today is an important day for all of Crimea, Ukraine and Russia." Manita spoke for hundreds of thousands of Crimeans; she wasn't alone. 66-year-old Vera Sverkunova sang "I want to go home to Russia. It's been so long since I've seen my mama." Apparently, the US government dismissed those happy voters as being held at gunpoint. I can't remember to have ever seen hundreds of thousands of people so happy being held at gunpoint.

Whatever one might think of Vladimir Putin the Russian President in regards to the crisis in Ukraine, it was even more difficult to understand the rationale for Obama's involvement. 1) Ukraine is in Russia's backyard 2) lawmakers in Crimea voted unanimously (78-0) to split from Ukraine and rejoin Russia 3) the People overwhelmingly (96%) voted for the annexation. While the "world" (translation the West: US, UK, Germany, etc.) might disagree of Russia' position or involvement or couldn't figure out Putin' endgame and was quite possibly unsure on the best course of action, it was however counterproductive for the United States in particular (or the West) to

even suggest sanctions against Russia,
let alone initiate the process.

Irrespective of the politics here at
home, it was a route the Obama
administration should have avoided at
all cost. First, the irrational
maneuver to establish sanctions was
more a bullying approach than
diplomacy; second, the approach opened
the door for hardliners in Putin's
administration to push their agendas
and open the wounds of the Cold War
era or even to pave the way for the
start of another one; third, there
were two major developments in the
Middle East which required Russia help
to bring those negotiations to a
successful conclusion: Syria and Iran,
both of which have good to strong
relations with Russia.

The Obama administration shouldn't
delude itself that Russia would simply

rollover and cooperate in those and future talks, especially after publicly slapping sanctions against Russian and pro-Russia Ukrainian officials; in fact, Vladimir Putin already promised to retaliate in kind against US sanctions. After more than 200 years on the world stage, the US government stills resorts to only one way to resolve conflicts: the use of force. Unfortunately, such option was not available in the Ukraine crisis. - *Russia could flex its muscles as much as US* - So, the US government resorted to the second best option: bullying. Sadly, that too was an approach that could not produce the intended result. In addition to having been wrong in its involvement in the Ukraine crisis, the US government resorted to the most expedient route (use of force, bullying) instead of using diplomacy. Unaware or unwilling to accept that the world has changed, the US government will continue to face other countries which can challenge its military power. Most unfortunately, ignorance is not an excuse and we Americans will pay hefty consequences for letting our government run amok.

In the 2012 State of the Union address, Mr. Obama promised "to do more nation building at home". He should have kept his promise. The US government should have stayed a neutral party in the Ukraine crisis. Besides the terrible mistake of getting involved, the sanctions against Russian and Ukrainian officials served no other purpose but to take the United States back to the cold war era.

For it's impossible to know, to anticipate or to predict how Obama's Russian counterpart would react.

Hardliners in Russia had dreamt of that very moment, and the Obama administration facilitated their reemergence in Russia political discourse. "Russia would not take orders from the United States, especially in matters that Russia deems critical to its national security." As it stood then, Ukraine was such a critical matter. No amount of sanctions imposed on Russia can change the dynamic in favor of the Obama administration. There were only two possible outcomes, neither of which seemed good.

1.- To isolate Russia – *from the West* - was to provide enough rationale for the hardliners to convince Putin to move forward with whatever plan he might have regarding the situation in Ukraine, including its occupation.

2.- To continue to be involved in the Ukraine crisis provided political opponents at home enough ammunition to label the administration as indecisive and weak. Well, that was already happening.

The options available to Obama then were very limited. If Putin were to move forward towards occupying Ukraine (or re-annexing it), there was really not much the US could do unless the country was willing to engage in war with Russia; I doubted very much Obama would have had the support of the American people to go to war with Russia over Ukraine. So, it was somewhat puzzling that the Obama administration created a situation which presented no benefit whatsoever.

Ukraine was at an impasse. Nothing but diplomacy, real diplomacy that is, could help craft a workable solution.

Sanctions, threat of sanctions, flexing of muscles, tough talk did much to exacerbate the situation, and the US government believes those are tools of diplomacy. Besides the fact that the US involvement in the crisis was not warranted, the Obama administration fully injected US government into the fray, took and defended one side and attached derogatory labels – terrorist – to the other side. It is always wrong, completely unwise for the US government to get involved in another country's domestic dispute. The Ukrainians reacted to the Obama administration meddling in their internal disputes, calling the Crimean terrorists, "We are all Ukrainians, and we are here to vote. We are not terrorists, said Irina, a Ukrainian voter – *opting for the annexation of Crimea* - during an interview with an

NBC News reporter, calling out US double standard.

No objective observer would have shrugged off the need for a resolution to the impasse in the Ukraine crisis; however, no logical person would have approved of the US involvement and approach as ways to solve the crisis either. As mentioned earlier, Russia's interest in the crisis was high and justified, not so for the United States. If the Obama administration was really serious about helping the Ukrainians, a) he would not have rushed to impose any sanction on Russian Officials b) he would have stopped the threats of more sanctions and the flexing of muscles c) he would have engaged in diplomacy.

Obama got a failing grade for his handling of the Ukraine crisis. If one follows the trajectory of the relation between the US and the Russia governments since, it should be obvious that both countries have drifted away more and more, heading towards the cold war era posture they both held. History would probably record that the start of World War III began when US became involved in the Ukraine crisis. That move by Obama was the scariest any president has made in a very longtime. Although he had since backed away from forcing the issue, the wheels of war did not stop however; in fact, they are still grinding, fast it seems.

Russia has already abandoned the accord (http://wapo.st/2fjXJAP) signed by both Obama and then Russian President Dmitry Medvedev for the reduction in nuclear weapons; US had just completed the installation of a new missile defense system (http://nyti.ms/2f1gc1B) in

Romania (*southeastern European country which shares borders with Ukraine*) in May 2016 and as recently as June 2016 NATO had engaged in the largest war game in eastern Europe since cold war according to The Guardian.

NATO War Game Exercise

The NATO exercise comprised 24 countries, over 30,000 troops, thousands of military vehicles and lasted ten days of tactical military exercise.

NATO Troops & Equipment

Russia did not sit idle; it did not spend its time complaining about the move by the US. Instead, Mr. Putin has been busy putting in place troops, warships, missiles and implementing war strategy maneuvers which closely resemble preparations for an imminent war.

According to an October 2016 article on USA Today, US Allies in Europe are deeply worried; Russia has not only intensified its missile exercise, it has deployed nuclear-capable missiles this month to its territory in the Baltic Sea.

Russian Warship Fires Missile

Even more troubling are increased talks about using nuclear weapons, more military maneuvers with nuclear arms, development of advanced nuclear munitions and public discussion of a new war doctrine. It seems that "Russia is exercising its military forces and its nuclear force more offensively than it used to do".

As pointed out earlier, all these developments are direct result of US involvement in the Ukraine crisis. It is impossible NOT to imagine that the escalation would continue to an extremely dangerous level for mankind.

Trump, Ukraine & Putin

The favorable opinion Mr. Trump has of Vladimir Putin and expressed over the course of several months during the presidential campaign has quite a few politicians worried. For decades and many US presidents (Republican & Democrat alike) the de facto relationship with Russia has been strategic at best and a cat and mouse game at the very least. Neither party trusts the other.

US has a capitalist system and Russia has a communist system; US government hates communism more than Russian government hates capitalism but both countries have been in a race to expand their respective doctrines to the farthest corner of the earth. They are arch enemies, with plenty of nuclear missile power. Both sides understand that an all-out war between them may doom the whole world. So, no matter what their disagreement is, they've always worked it out somehow. They have been keeping one another at arm's length however; more often than not, Russia would offer a carrot stick to US and observe the behavior. More often than not, US would always take the bait and would act badly. Such was the case with the Libya carrot stick (test) dangling in front of Obama by the Russian president. After resetting relation with Russia's Dmitry Medvedev, then Russia's president, the Obama administration got a pass (from Russia), attacked Libya and toppled its ruler Muammar Gaddafi.

Russia didn't complain but when its government went into Crimea, Ukraine to quell uprising in the country and in the process annexed Crimea into Russia, the US government quickly condemned the move and imposed sanctions on some Russian and (complicit) Ukrainian officials. US position on the issue contributed to a rapid deterioration of US-Russia relation. Mr. Putin took the opportunity to scrap nuclear disarmament agreement with US and began a race which is very reminiscent of the cold war era. Obama's unwillingness to revisit the issue led him to "slap" further sanctions on Russia mere weeks before he exited the Oval Office.

On a parallel track, Donald Trump continued to advance that he will win the general elections – *despite trailing Mrs. Clinton by double digit at the time* - and leave the door open to have a friendly relation with Vladimir Putin, a position which pleased Mr. Putin greatly. To ensure Trump's victory in the general election, Mr. Putin instructed hackers - *according to US intelligence reports* - in Russia to find, extract and release derogatory information about Trump's opponent, Hillary Clinton.

Russian hackers obliged; in addition, it didn't help Hillary's candidacy that FBI director James Comey dropped a bombshell about Hillary's emails with just a few days before the voting.

As President Elect, Mr. Trump continued to promote the idea of a friendly relation with Russia; he even suggested he would consider removing the sanctions imposed by the Obama

administration on Russia.
Interestingly, most Republicans not
only applauded Obama move (to put
sanctions on Russia) but also
criticized him for not going further.
So, Mr. Trump's position on Russia is
diametrically opposed to Republicans';
what could be the most plausible
explanation for Mr. Trump NOT to let
the status quo remain vis-à-vis
Russia?

The answer is perhaps much simpler
than the question is complicated. Mr.
Trump has done business in Russia but
most importantly it seems, according
to some reports, that the Russian
government either partners with or
invests in Trump's operation. Some
even suggest that the Russian
government, perhaps Vladimir Putin
himself, is heavily invested in
Trump's operation. The theory seems

plausible, considering that Mr. Trump has gone out of his way to avoid upsetting Mr. Putin or at the very least defending him.

If that is indeed the case, one can easily conclude that Mr. Trump would not confront Russia if Mr. Putin were to decide to go further into Ukraine or even attempt to move into other regions of the world which were once considered off limit for Russia by the West.

As president of the United States, Mr. Trump has a lot of flexibility when it comes to foreign relations; as such, his coziness with Russia is not to be discarded as mere trumpism for, as it seems, Mr. Trump is unknowingly re-shaping the world geopolitics.

Will that be good for the United States? Perhaps! After all, the world

leader would become responsible –
financially – for everything which
occurs. While such changes might strip
US of its leadership role, the country
may become financially more prosperous
since it will be able to invest in the
country instead of distributing
taxpayers' money to foreign
governments.

This page is intentionally left blank

UNEMPLOYMENT

When Obama took office in January
2009, the US unemployment rate was at
a national average of 9.3%; the rate
was even higher in 14 states
(including California, Florida,
Illinois, North Carolina and Florida);
those states' unemployment rate was
10% or higher. The country was
shedding jobs at a monthly average of
250,000. According to a report
published in November 2008 by the
Economic Policy Institute (EPI), –
*just two months prior to Obama
assuming the presidency* – there were
already over ten million (10,000,000)
people unemployed in the country, and
the projected monthly unemployment
estimates gave no reason to smile
either; the country would continue to

shed jobs in the next few months at the same rate (or more rapidly).

Ironically, Republican Legislators in Washington were smiling. - *I did not make that up* - Despite the fact that Obama inherited the economic recession, they were very elated; they saw an opportunity to make good on Mitch McConnell's promise "to make Obama a one-term president"; they saw a silver lining for the Republican Party. The Republican strategists believed that the longer the recession lasted the better it was for the Party, for a long recession would provide the Party ample time to cast Obama as a failed president. To that end, Republican Legislators were hard at work setting roadblocks for the president. To the detriment of the unemployed and at the cost of the country falling further into the

recession, the GOP Representatives -
*whose primary concern should have been
to work with the president to revive
the economy* - devised a strategy, not
to help getting people back to work
but to reframe the discussion, to
paint Obama as ineffective and
incompetent. The strategy was several
fold a) to blame the president for not
doing enough to create jobs b) to
constantly block whatever the
president tried to do to remedy the
situation c) to convince the
Republican constituents that Obama
created the problem. To most analysts'
surprise, their strategy worked, with
some help from the Party mouthpiece of
course, Fox Opinion, - *known and
referred to by most as Fox News* - Rush
Limbaugh, Ann Coulter et al.

One must not be deluded into believing
that Obama' overwhelming popularity

which got him elected as the first black president was a rallying cry for unity. Republicans have long proven to be anti-minority, anti-black; the election of Barack Obama was neither a capitulation of the Republican Party nor an acceptance for blacks' integration.

In fact, polls taken Jan 21-25 2009 put the president at just 41% job approval rating among Republicans; although the polls were completely irrelevant and could not possibly have anything to do with the new president, it should shed some light on the Republican electorate. Just five days into the presidency, his job approval rating didn't even reach 50. Barack Obama was sworn into office in January 20, 2009. Obviously, polls taken the next four days couldn't possibly provide any useful information as far as Obama's job approval, and yet, the GOP constituents couldn't bring themselves to even give the guy a chance to prove himself. At the end of 2009, Obama approval rating among Republicans was at 16% (shocking huh!) and had continued to slide down to single digit. The last poll per this writing (Jun 20-26 2016) placed the president at just 11% approval rating among Republicans. Surely, GOP Representatives have done a very effective job brainwashing the Republican constituents to dislike the president but there is one area they couldn't prevail, in the facts. No matter how much GOP leaders hated Obama, they could not change the facts. As of the revision of this book, the unemployment rate stood at just 4.7% according to the Bureau of Labor Statistics News Release on June 3, 2016.

Although the GOP Representatives (as well as the constituents) have plenty to be thankful about in regards to Obama's leadership, they've continued to "dog him" regarding the job market. Republicans Leaders could not come to grip that despite their nefarious and malicious attitude towards the president and their constant opposition towards him, he had prevailed.

It is one thing to hate an individual but it's unpatriotic, bordering betrayal to gamble the fate of a whole country in order to score political points, and yet still lose. That has to sting a little bit, well a lot. But what was even most puzzling is the fact that the Republican constituents were unable to set aside their hatred for Obama to acknowledge they too had

benefited of his leadership in regards
to the job market. However, when GOP
leaders were asked whether they were
patriots, they considered the question
insulting. They did not find it
unpatriotic to work against the
wellbeing of the country; they could
not comprehend that to deliberately
push the country further into
recession in order to get rid of Obama
was betrayal. - Reflection: *I do
ponder sometimes whether Republican
Leaders are deprived of a functioning
brain. Has their hatred for Obama
stripped them all of a rational mind?
Or has their hatred blinded them? A
logical mind, it seems, is unnecessary
to belong to the Republican Party* -
Below is a chart from the Bureau of
Labor Statistics which provides a
glimpse of the state of the job market
(8% + unemployment rate) when Obama
assumed the presidency in January 2009

and the state of the job market as of November 2015 (4.7% unemployment rate) just a year before Obama's presidency comes to an end.

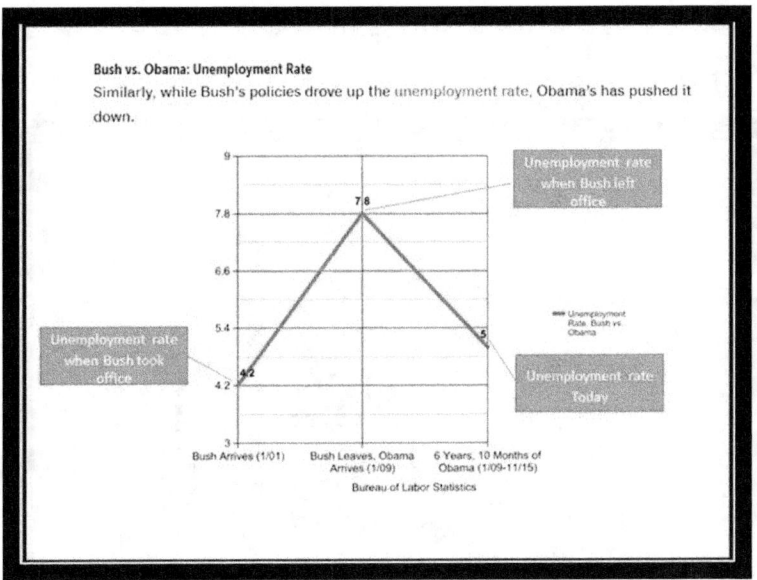

As it should be evident, when Obama assumed the presidency in January 2009, the country was hemorrhaging jobs at a dizzying rate (*462,000 in January 2009 alone, the very month Obama was sworn into office*). By November 2015 (*just one year before*

the end of his second term), the Obama
administration had recorded net
private sector jobs created slightly
under 13 million (13,000,000) as
displayed in the chart below.

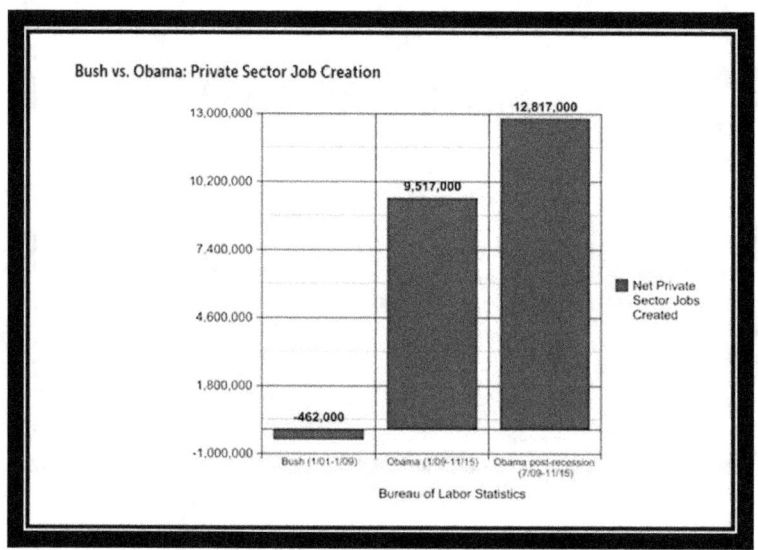

This information is available to
anyone; they were provided by the same
agency (*Bureau of Labor Statistics*)
responsible to collect these types of
information under every president. No
need to argue (with me) regarding the

facts. The facts are the facts. As previously stated, Republicans in general have a history of arguing with and against facts. And if and when it becomes obvious they're losing the argument, they would turn the discussion about the validity and/or accuracy of the facts. Can you see the oxymoron sign flashing? Facts are verifiable; therefore, they cannot be invalid or inaccurate. For instance, if I say that all men are mortal, I stated a fact. There is no way around it; if someone can prove that even "one" man is immortal my statement can no longer be construed as fact. I hope I clear this matter once and for all.

It is very difficult to grasp the justification any Republican leader who aspires to become president would have to deceive the constituents he wishes to lead someday as commander in chief; but it is even more troubling that the constituents are so gullible, so ignorant of the current state of affairs. It is troubling they are so uninformed or misinformed of what's going on in their own country. It could be that hatred' side effect is to destroy the brain or to deprive it of rational ability. One doesn't have to like an athlete or a team to acknowledge his performance or superiority, would you agree? So, it would not matter that Republicans didn't like Obama; his accomplishments - *lower unemployment rate, Obamacare, lower debt, lower expenditures, economic recovery, etc.* - are FACTS. It seems as if the Republican Party in its entirety is under some sort of spell which deprives its members of the simplest form of "logical reasoning."

Enter Trump

Mr. Trump is convinced that the low unemployment (4.6%) rate published by the Department of Labor during the presidential campaigns was fake; at least, that was what then candidate Trump advanced. According to him, "The unemployment rate is probably 20 percent, but I will tell you, you have some great economists that will tell you it's a 30, 32. And the highest I've heard so far is 42 percent."

Although it's certain Mr. Trump was wrong about the rate, he was also wrong about the rate he claimed some economists advanced but that's no longer important; he is now the president of the United States. He ran most of his campaign with the promise to bring back jobs in America, at a rate such that people would be asking

him to stop. Whether that would be the
case or not is not important. Mr.
Trump has always prided himself to
know better than anyone on planet
Earth how to do this, that and the
other. For him to keep his promise and
to succeed would be welcome news to
the country.

This page is intentionally left blank

ECONOMY

When former Senator John Kerry who later served as Secretary of State in Obama administration during his second term as president of the United States bid for the office of the presidency in 2004, he used a famous line – *which coincidentally was and is still true –* in an attempt to appeal to the electorate, mostly Independents and Republicans whose focus and priority might have been the economy, "if you want to live like a Republican, you should elect a Democrat." Although his call did not produce the intended result, to elect him as president of the United States, – *the country was mostly still focused on security after the September 11, 2001 attacks on US soil by bin Laden; just a year earlier George W. Bush started a war with*

Iraq; although the war was under false pretexts, the revelation of the Bush administration deception was still under wrap – John Kerry made a valid point which is in fact supported by statistics. For the past six decades, positive economic performance has been mostly under Democratic presidents. US News reported on October 2015 in an article that "four of the five presidents who have overseen the largest average economic expansions since World War II have been Democrats – John F. Kennedy, Lyndon B. Johnson, Bill Clinton and Jimmy Carter".

While it is common practice for any Republican aspiring to the presidency to promise better economic future for all, history is yet to record much economic success under Republican presidency. It was disingenuous, outright deceiving for Republicans to suggest that the economy was worse under Obama than it was under George W. Bush; ironically and most troubling is the fact that the Republican constituents actually believed that was the case. *I must admit that I have given up trying to understand this phenomenon.* The data are available, the proofs some of which are current, verifiable and yet the Republican Party as a whole believed just the opposite. It's a mystery which simply cannot be deciphered.

When Obama took office in 2009, the country was in a grim recession; in addition to a job market in free fall, the financial sector – *fondly or grudgingly referred to as Wall Street* – contributed to worsen the situation; it literally brought the country to its knees. Every major sector in the country – *auto industry, real estate, manufacture, technology, etc.* - was affected. Policies which were enacted under the Bush administration gave green light to funds' managers to gamble consumers' savings, retirement funds and investments; and funds' managers didn't disappoint; they gleefully obliged. The result was a complete financial meltdown in 2008 at the very end of the Bush presidency. Obama took office in January 2009; six years into his presidency, not only has the economy recovered somewhat but corporate profits have also more than doubled (*see the graph below*). That doesn't mean everything was rosy; when has it ever been? However, there was no comparison between the Obama administration and the Bush's in regards to the economy. See the graph below which shows how corporate profits have skyrocketed under the Obama administration.

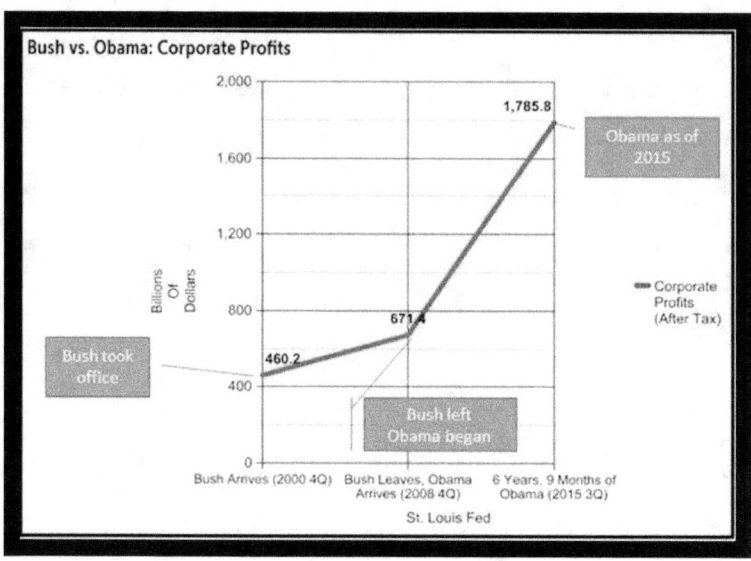

As illustrated in the graph, when Bush exited the presidency, corporate profits were at approximately $671 billion; that was fantastic (*for the corporate world of course*) considering that the rest of the country was struggling to get by but when Obama took office, a few short years later, corporate profits soared; by the third quarter of the year 2015, corporate profits were recorded at $1.8

trillion, almost twice as much as during the Bush administration. So, how does one reconcile the argument that the Obama administration was against small businesses all the while enacted policies and provided the platform for such huge profits? One cannot. It was an argument which was only valid in the minds of the Republicans but the "facts" told a very different story. Granted that politicians in general Republican politicians in particular have mastered the art of spinning information, it was nevertheless puzzling, especially in the age of digital information that the Republican electorate were unable to separate facts from fabricated stories pushed unto them by their Representatives.

Trump's Plan

Throughout his campaign, Mr. Trump had
complained repeatedly about the slow
growth of the US economy, *"We're dying
at 1% GDP growth; we don't make things
anymore"* Mr. Trump mentioned
throughout his campaign. For the
record, the US economy growth rate
stands at 3.5% as of the third quarter
in 2016. Although that last number is
better than 1%, Mr. Trump made his
observation in comparison to India
(growing at 8%) and China (growing at
7%); here is how his plan to change
all that was described on his website
*"GDP is at 1% now, and if [Hillary]
got in, it will be less than zero. But
we're bringing it from 1% up to 4%.
And I actually think [with my economic
plan] we can go higher than 4%. I
think you can go to 5% or 6%. And if
we do, you don't have to bother asking*

[about jobs], because we have a tremendous machine. We will have created a tremendous economic machine once again. To do that, we're taking back jobs. We're not going to let our companies be raided by other countries where we lose all our jobs, we don't make our product anymore."

Although Mr. Trump never offers any specific on how he would manage to increase the growth rate, there seems to be one recurring theme he believes would do the trick, it is to bring manufacturing jobs back into the country. It is indeed recognized that less unemployment is better for the economy, that's the good news but in everything in life, one has to give something to get something back. It so happens Mr. Trump proposes to give a lot

a) reduce corporate taxes to a bare minimum, and even eliminate taxes in some cases

b) increase the country debt by 28% (currently at 77% of GDP; will jump to 105% when Trump's policy is factored in) according to the nonpartisan Committee for a Responsible Federal Budget. Trump's answer: "Well, I say they're wrong…"

c) the unspoken side effect: We The People will have to foot up the bill for all government expenses.

It is too early to collect data generated by Mr. Trump' policy. In a year (or so), it should be obvious whether Mr. Trump's plan to bring jobs back works.

This page is intentionally left blank

EXPENDITURES

Remember the 2012 Obama bid for re-
election? Maybe not. But what you
probably remember is the famous 47%
statement (http://bit.ly/2isboGC) by Mitt
Romney? No? Well, that's okay. Let me
refresh your memory. In the 2012 bid
for the presidency, Mitt Romney,
former Governor of Massachusetts
challenged Obama, then the incumbent
president; the prize was of course the
Oval Office. The stakes were high for
Obama; the country was in the worst
economic state ever. After almost
three years in office, Obama was able
to slow down a bit the hemorrhage in
the job market but there were plenty
of signs the bleeding didn't stop; in
fact, one could say there was still
internal bleeding. There were plenty
of signs everywhere that the miracle

(financial recovery) the country
expected from Savior Obama didn't
happen, yet.

To make matters worse, the Republican
led Congress which had worked
tirelessly to block everything Obama
tried to achieve, saw a golden
opportunity to help Mitch McConnell
fulfill his congressional "duty" (*the
sacred goal he set for himself on
Obama's inauguration day*) to make
Obama a one-term president. Yes, you
read correctly; to the detriment of
the constituents (*whether you were
Democrat or Republican, you would pay
the same price, you would suffer the
same consequences*), the Republican
Representatives in Washington did not
only refuse to help Obama turn the
economy around but they also stood on
his way to prevent him from making any

progress towards achieving such, to improve the economy.

Republicans in Washington give patriotism a bad name. How does one claim to be a patriot and at the same work against the wellbeing of the country? That was ironically how the Republican Representatives manifested their patriotism. Imagine for a moment that you are hired to do a job; you are provided no tool, no resource, no help. In addition, imagine that your employer also ties your hands (literally), betting there will be plenty of opportunities to say you're not capable of doing the job; you are incompetent. Visualize that scenario for just a second. How could you do the job for which you would be hired? Well, that was precisely the predicament Republican Representatives put Obama in; that was exactly what

the Republicans in Washington expected
to happen to the president, he would
be unable to do the job the American
people entrusted him to do.
Interestingly, luckily or ironically,
Obama had performed the most jaw-
dropping magical act or the biggest
political stunt in history, – *Even
Harry Houdini would have had to learn
a thing or two from Obama* – he had
managed to perform the job (*with both
hands tied*) for which he was hired
better than even those whose hands
were completely free, were provided
all the tools and resources as well as
assistance when needed. There lies the
root of the frustration expressed by
the Republican legislators in
Washington. Despite having set
political roadblocks everywhere, Obama
had managed to get a lot done without
a single Republican being able to

claim credit for helping. That has to sting.

According to the Congressional Budget Office (CBO), - *CBO is strictly nonpartisan; it conducts objective, impartial analysis; and hires its employees solely on the basis of professional competence without regard to political affiliation. CBO does not make policy recommendations, and each report and cost estimate summarizes the methodology underlying the analysis* - expenditures under Obama have been flat, not only in comparison to the Bush administration but also in contrast to prophet Ronald Reagan, the 40th president of the United States (1981- 1989). The combined chart below displays an interesting contrast between the Obama administration and several previous administrations.

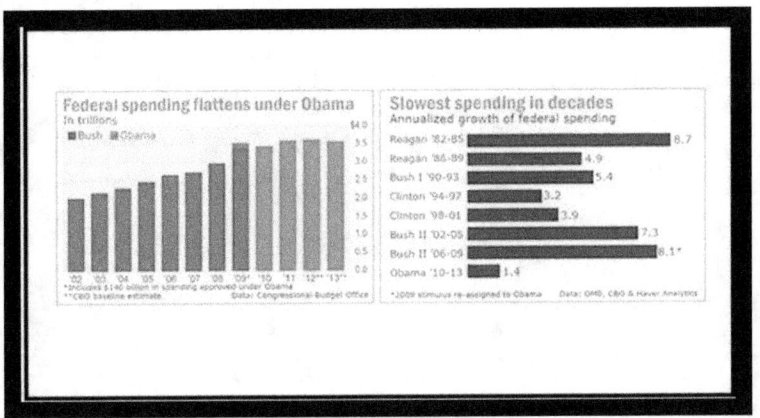

If you're not good in math, the graph
above should give you a pretty good
understanding of Obama' spending
habit; even if you're wearing your
Republican glasses, it should be
obvious (*even to a blind man perhaps*)
that there are more expenditures which
occur under Republican administrations
in general than under Democrats'. For
instance, under Ronald Reagan, in his
first term in office as president,
federal spending was 8.7 percent;
under Bush I, federal spending was 5.4
percent; under Bush II, federal

spending was 7.3 percent. By contrast, under Bill Clinton, federal spending was 3.2 percent and under Obama in his first term, federal spending was just 1.4 percent. Those are facts.

So, if the Republican constituents were really, seriously concerned about government spending, they would have stopped voting for Republican Representatives (and presidents) to send to Washington. They would have abandoned the Republican doctrine completely and fled the Republican Party altogether. Otherwise, they should all stop the pretext that they care about government spending. As it stands today, according to the FACTS, Republican administrations have spent much, much more than Democratic administrations.

Case in point, when Bill Clinton'
presidency ended in 2000, the country
inherited a budget surplus of almost
$2 trillion dollars ($1.9T to be
exact) thanks to the economic policy
his administration implemented.
However, in his first year in office,
yes the very first year (*the first 12
months of the administration*) George
W. Bush wiped out the whole surplus.
At the end of his presidency, George
W. Bush left the country with $800
billion dollars deficit, according to
"The Hill". Although Republicans are
always quick to point out that Obama's
deficit is double that of George W.
Bush, one must factor in the surplus
he inherited to arrive at the true
deficit under his administration. In
essence, Bush squandered $2 trillion
dollars in surplus and ran a deficit
of $800 billion dollars which bring
the true deficit under George W. Bush

to $2.8 trillion dollars. Republicans
should stop the pretext that they care
about government spending; they DO
NOT.

It is also worth noting that the
conclusion drawn by the Congressional
Budget Office in regards to
expenditures under the Obama
administration was also shared by the
Bureau of Economic Analysis (BEA) -
*Source of US economic statistics
including national income and product
accounts (NIPAs), gross domestic
product ... The BEA Advisory Committee
advises the Director of BEA on matters
related to the development and
improvement of BEA's national,
regional, industry, and international
economic accounts, especially in areas
of new and rapidly growing economic
activities arising from innovative and
advancing technologies, and provides*

recommendations from the perspectives
of the economics profession, business,
and government. - The chart below
shows a contrast in spending habit
between the Reagan administration and
the Obama's.

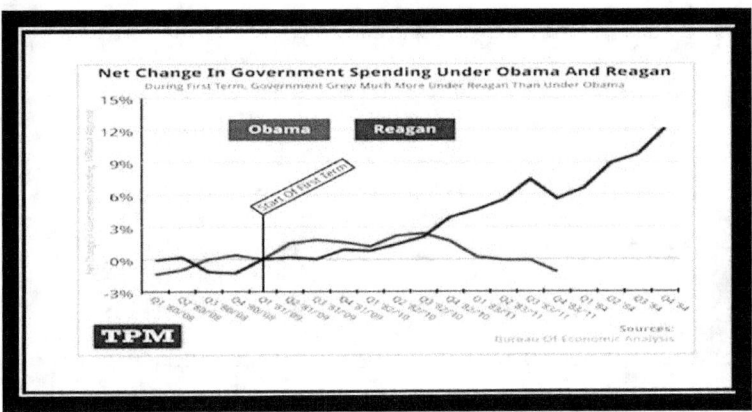

As it should be quite obvious by now,
Republican Legislators' outrage over
Obama' alleged outlandish spending is
unwarranted, theatrical and spreading
rumors to this regard is outright
deceptive. Republican Legislators make
it their mission to argue with facts,
distort them and offer their

electorate a picture of the state of
the government which only exists in
their narrative; also unfortunately,
the Republican electorate have always
chosen the "fact free" reality which
might contribute to making Washington
what it's always been, a place where
nothing is done.

Either the Republicans are confused
between fact and fabrication, they
might think both are the same or they
simply don't care. The chart above –
*provided by the Bureau of Economic
Analysis* – shows both the Obama and
the Reagan administration at the start
of their respective first terms in
office (*look where it says START OF
FIRT TERM*). As you can see, at the end
of Reagan's first term presidency in
1984, spending has gone way up, all
the way to 12%; by contrast, at the
end of Obama's third year in his first

term presidency, spending fell below zero (0); yes, you read correctly, below zero. It did go slightly up to 1.4% the following year (2012). That was great performance considering that Obama operated under one of the worst economic recessions.

Trump's Solution

Spend less. As a businessman, Mr. Trump's approach to being profitable is very simple: make more, spend less. Can such approach be duplicated at the government's level? Mr. Trump seems to believe so.

During an interview with MSNBC Chuck Todd on October 4, 2015, Mr. Trump proposed to a) cut defense budget b) eliminate entire departments:

Environment Protection Agency (EPA) &
Dept. of Education were the two
mentioned. His logic is that he would
eliminate waste and cut expenses
wherever there is room to do so. Per
his belief, both EPA & the Department
of Education represent government
wastes.

Ironically, his cabinet includes:

1) Rick Perry as Secretary of
   Energy, the same agency Trump
   said is a waste, the same agency
   Rick Perry proposed to eliminate
   when he bid for the presidency of
   the United States in 2012 during
   a debate

2) Betsy Devos as Secretary of
   Education, the other agency he
   considers a waste which he
   proposed to eliminate.

So, how does Trump propose to cut
expenses? Does it matter?

This page is intentionally left blank

DEBT

One of the most frequently used political tool by candidates vying for the Oval Office is the National Debt. In general, Republicans are usually most successful in their marketing, not because their arguments are correct but rather because they're smarter than Democrats. Republicans are much better at selling to the electorate the "fear of having to pay for expenses which could be avoided" and would become financial burden for the future generations. If you've been paying very close attention to US politics, you would notice that Republicans in general would always bring the topic (of National Debt) for discussion – *during presidential campaigns and debates* – when a Democratic president occupies the Oval

Office but would usually shy away from it when the occupant in the Oval Office is a Republican. The reason is actually a very simple one, - *as illustrated in the chart below* - national debt rises drastically under Republican administrations. No, this is not a typo, you read correctly. This is what we call FACTS.

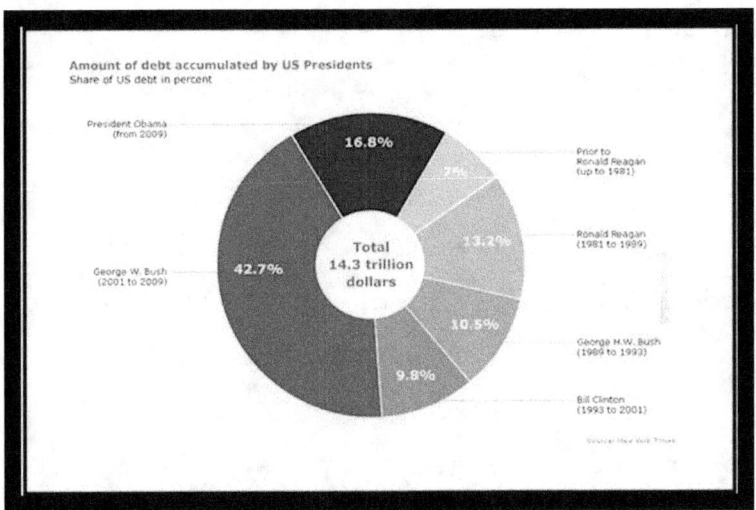

Amount of debt accumulated by US Presidents
Share of US debt in percent

President Obama (from 2009) — 16.8%

Prior to Ronald Reagan (up to 1981) — 7%

Ronald Reagan (1981 to 1989) — 13.2%

George W. Bush (2001 to 2009) — 42.7%

Total 14.3 trillion dollars

George H.W. Bush (1989 to 1993) — 10.5%

Bill Clinton (1993 to 2001) — 9.8%

Source: New York Times

It actually makes sense. Under Democratic administrations, much less is spent than under Republican counterparts. Spending and Debt have a very direct (1:1) correlation; as more expenses occur without the ability to pay for those expenses, one's debt increases. The principle is the same for the country as it is for your own personal finance. The more you spend using your credit cards, the more you owe; that's as simple as that. It so happens that under Republican administrations, more expenditures happen.

As illustrated in the chart earlier, under George W. Bush, the debt rose to 42.7%; actually, it was much worse than the number itself. George W. Bush inherited a budget surplus of almost $2 trillion dollars when he assumed the presidency.

The reason you may not know that is because 1) as mentioned previously,

Republicans are usually "mum" when they're in control of the political machines in Washington 2) they only raise the issue when Democrats are in control, thus giving you the impression that Democrats are irresponsible when it comes to national debt 3) Democrats are not comfortable using simple slogans to explain such a complex issue.
Are Democrats simply stupid or conscientious?

It's the latter. In fact, it is true that national debt is not a topic which can be discussed using a slogan or even in a presidential debate where only a few minutes are allocated for the discussion. Since Republicans have no qualm scaring the bejesus out of everyone and they're more concerned about scoring political points, they make use of any tool that's available.

In addition, it's worth mentioning that Republicans don't care an iota about national debt. How could I possibly know that? If indeed they were a) the issue would not have been buried when they're in control during which time they could actually do something about the debt b) they would not have contributed to increase it – *at times drastically* – when they're in control.

So, it is quite logical to conclude the only reason they bring it up when they're not in control is to scare the electorate, deceive them and give them a reason NOT to vote for Democrats. The chart above which clearly shows the contrast between Republicans and Democrats in terms of spending habit was provided by the New York times; one could argue about its accuracy; it could be wrong; it could be biased.

However, the chart below was provided
by the Treasury Department

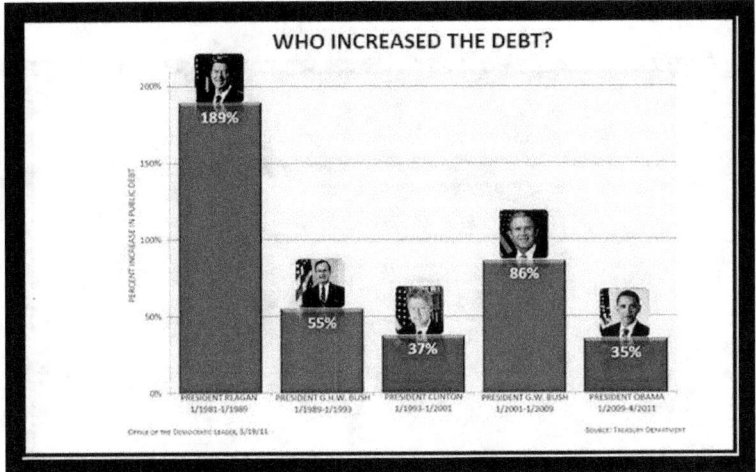

Fig 2

The graph in Fig 2 reflects the debt
accumulated under the Obama
administration up to April 2011, more
than a year before the expiration of
his first term presidency; the graph
below (Fig 3) provides a more
comprehensive view of the spending
habits of past presidents up to the
end of Obama administration first
term. Fig 3 displays how much is spent

by each administration at the end of
their respective first terms in
office.

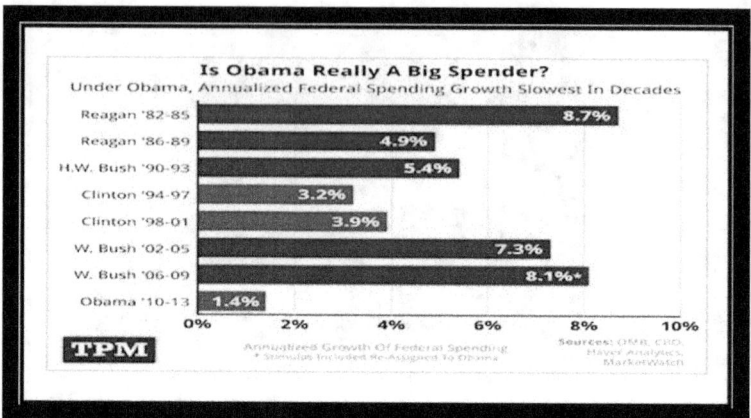

Fig 3

These data were provided by the Office
of Management and Budget (OMB)
supported by the Congressional Budget
Office (CBO), both of which are
independent agencies which operate
under both major (or all) political
Parties.

As previously stated, the national
debt is a very complex issue; although

it is factually correct that Obama administration's debt is in par with other previous administrations, meaning no better no worse, - *except George W. Bush whose debt in his first term in office almost tripled the average of several previous administrations combined, as seen in the chart above.* - Republicans have always mixed various components of the debt in the debate to confuse the constituents; and they really want to confuse them because it works to their advantage politically. National Debt in general should be discussed in conjunction with the Gross Domestic Product (GDP) which is calculated as follows:

$GDP = C + G + I + NX$

C is equal to all private consumption, or consumer spending, in a nation's economy, G is the sum of government spending, I is the sum of all the country's investments, including businesses capital expenditures and NX is the nation's total net exports, calculated as total exports minus total imports (NX = Exports - Imports). Without bogging you down with the intricate details in the calculation of the GDP and its correlation with the national debt, the presence of government spending (G) factor in the GDP calculation should trigger the flag of national debt changes.

Trump Hates Debt

So he says! He rants so much about the national debt one would think he has aversion for debt. Shortly after announcing his candidacy for the presidency of the United States, Mr.

Trump said the following on June 16, 2015 *"If we have another 3 or 4 years--we're at $8 trillion now--we're soon going to be at $20 trillion. According to the economists--who I'm not big believers in, but, nevertheless, this is what they're saying--that $24 trillion--we're very close--that's the point of no return. $24 trillion. We will be there soon. That's when we become Greece. That's when we become a country that's unsalvageable. And we're gonna be there very soon. We're gonna be there very soon."*

It cannot possibly be emphasized more than Mr. Trump has, debt is bad. According to experts however, the very economic policies he is now proposing would increase debt by a whopping 28% of the current amount. - *in other words, if Mr. Trump's policy is implemented, the national debt will*

increase to 25.6%, from $20T to $25.6T
irrespective of whether Trump wins a
second term or not –

One should not be so surprised; Mr.
Trump has built his empire almost
exclusively on debt and on more than
five occasions he filed bankruptcy.
One can only hope that maybe, just
maybe Mr. Trump has learned from his
mistakes.

This page is intentionally left blank

SOCIAL ISSUES

Be it by coincidence or deliberate, Obama will probably be known historically as the President of the "Firsts". He is already (recognized as) the first black President since the creation of the Republic. And when it comes to social issues, Obama has done everything possible to be the first to tackle issues most administration would not even consider let alone make a priority.

He is the first president who has successfully implemented universal healthcare (well, a version of it), not without problems however. Even as of this writing, a Damocles sword stills hangs over the fate of Obamacare. The Republican led Congress voted over 50 times (54 to be exact, as of this writing) to repeal the Act, and if Donald Trump were to become president, he promised to shred Obamacare on Day One. Having said that, Mr. Obama is nevertheless the first president who has successfully implemented Universal Healthcare for all.

Dancing with the Sexes

Obama is also fondly referred to as the first LGBT president. No, he is not gay. His relentless fight for minority rights has also factored Lesbians, Gay Bi-Sexual and Transgender (LGBT) who have spent a great deal of their lives hiding their true sexual inclinations and gender identity.

The issue of homosexuals' rights has been debated for decades here in the United States. Bill Clinton, 42nd president, signed an executive order (*don't ask don't tell*) to shield anyone (*in the Armed Forces*) who didn't specifically reveal his/her sexual orientation from any punishment but it was Obama who has not only ended the practice of discrimination against homosexuals serving in the Armed Forces (*by repealing "don't ask don't tell"*) but also signed an executive LGBT non-discrimination order "barring discrimination on the basis of sexual orientation or gender identity among federal contractors.

The order also protects all federal employees from discrimination on the basis of gender identity" as reported on the July 21, 2014 article in Slate.com.

In order to circumvent Bill Clinton "don't ask don't tell" order, a number of States had moved to ban same-sex marriage; at the end of Bill's presidency in 2000, 31 states had passed law to ban same sex marriage. The number of states banning same sex marriage had continued to increase gradually as George W. Bush assumed the presidency in 2001. Interestingly in 2003, the state of Massachusetts – *the first to have done so* – passed law to legalize same sex marriage. Five years later in 2008, the state of Connecticut followed suit. When Obama assumed the presidency in 2009, it would be just a matter of time before same sex marriage became legal.

Even before the US Supreme Court ruled that the US Constitution guarantees the right for same-sex couples to marry in all 50 US states on June 26, 2015, a number of States had already opened their doors to same sex marriage, giving all married couples (heterosexual and homosexual alike) the same rights, benefits and privileges that were originally reserved to heterosexual couples only. While there are still many states – *in overwhelmingly Republican territory* – that have continued to resist the Supreme Court ruling, public pressure has forced government officials of those states (Governors, Senators) from passing laws or implementing policies which could have singled out homosexuals and penalized them. For instance, in North Carolina, a boycott (http://wp.me/p1yu17-yL) of various business activities (*entertainment, travel, shopping*) by visitors and residents alike have made it impossible to enforce the law which would have forced transgender to use the bathroom which identifies with their physical sexual organs. Even law enforcement officers have backed away from trying to enforce the Governor's order.

Tangling With Prisoners

President Obama at the El Reno Prison Facility conversing with Four Prisoners

Since the creation of the Republic, no sitting president has ever visited a prison; Obama is the first. On July 2015, the president of the United States made a historic visit to a federal prison. I can only imagine the level of scrutiny that facility must have undergone by Secret Service and the level of security which had to be in place before the president's visit; after all, it is an environment where even some criminals fear for their lives. Regardless, Obama toured the El Reno prison in Oklahoma City; he sat down with half a dozen inmates, the luckiest criminals on the planet, at the very least in the United States. The president brought attention to the fact that the prison population has more than quadrupled since 1980. Mr. Obama called for reforms in the criminal justice system in which non-violent criminals are not locked up for the rest of their lives behind bars. Mr. Obama stated that those individuals need to be rehabilitated, not incarcerated. The president noted that it is in the best interest of the States and of the country to rehabilitate those individuals (the non-violent criminals); Mr. Obama added that in addition to decreasing the prison population, such approach would also reduce the amount of money the government has to spend to sustain those facilities. – *At an average of $60 per day for each prisoner, it costs the State almost $22,000 ($21,900) per prisoner per year; rehabilitation for the same prisoner would have cost the taxpayers less than $10,000 –*

The president met with non-violent drug offenders who are sentenced to die behind bars; in an effort to jump start the process of changes to the criminal justice system, he commuted the sentence of 46 inmates and proposed to continue doing so till the end of his second term in office. As of June 2016, the president had commuted the sentences of well over 340 prisoners and as of August 2016, he has shortened the sentences of more

than 200 prisoners. Obama reflected
during his visit that, as a black man
in America, he could have wound up in
jail.

The president's visit marked an
important time in history; it outlined
how deeply embedded racism has been in
American culture. A study by major
universities and independent
organizations have shown there are as
many Whites who have used drugs as
there are Blacks and yet the prison
population is overwhelmingly filled
with minority offenders. 100+ years
after the abolition of slavery, Blacks
are still shackled; they are still
discriminated against; they are still
denied a good education; they are
still denied a good job; they are
still denied a promotion; they are
still at the bottom of the financial

ladder. They are still denied equal treatment in the justice system.

It is hopeful that the Obama's visit to a prison and the announcement by the Department of Justice to transfer the management of the prison facilities to the States will help decrease the injustice towards the Black community in particular. If nothing else, Obama opened the door for a more equitable justice system. It remains to be seen how much his effort would be strengthened by future administrations.

This page is intentionally left blank

SECURITY & TERRORISM

Whenever the topic of terrorism & security arises, most Republicans are always quick to suggest there was no act of terrorism in the United States until Obama assumed the presidency; some (*mostly hosts and guests on Fox Opinion including Mr. Giuliani of all people, former mayor of NY who was in office when the tragedy occurred*) overlooked that the tragedy of 9/11/2001 occurred under the Bush administration. There are even jokes which suggest that Obama was somewhat responsible for 9/11/2001 anyway, just for being Obama.

Notwithstanding the fact that 9/11 could have been avoided – *according to many sources at the Central Intelligence Agency (CIA)* - and there were plenty of acts of terrorism in US during the Bush administration (read details on politifact (http://bit.ly/2i5quyM), dailykos (http://bit.ly/2itHXju), mediamatters (http://mm4a.org/2hezQ9a) etc., the most important point is ignored in the partisan-driven arguments; both Bush (*after 9/11*) and Obama had managed to keep major terrorist tragedies from being inflicted on the homeland. However, regardless the measure taken by those whose job is to protect the country, one must recognize there is no system of security which can prevent individual acts of terrorism from happening 100% of the time, especially here in the United States where anyone can acquire a machine gun even on the internet. No president can claim to be able to prevent individual and isolated cases of terrorism regardless of the security strategy in place.

Determined to Restore America's Greatness

So the argument – *in regards to domestic acts of terrorism which have occurred during Obama's presidency –* is at best misleading considering the drastic increase in firearm purchases since Obama has assumed the presidency. Domestic terrorism aside, the Obama administration has done in its second year in office what the Bush administration couldn't accomplish in eight years; he dedicated enough resources and made it a priority to find and kill Osama bin Laden, the individual who was believed to have been responsible for the worst terrorist attacks on US soil, the 9/11/2001 attacks.

Before Obama, the electorate were more inclined to elect a Republican candidate as president of the United States, especially when matters of security were at stake; Republicans

were perceived more effective than
Democrats regarding external threats
to US. Obama has completely changed
the political landscape when it comes
to ensuring the security of the
homeland. Having killed the believed
mastermind behind the 9/11 attacks and
having pursued a relentless campaign
against leaders of terrorist groups
across the globe, Obama has chipped
away, considerably, the idea that a
Republican is needed in the Oval
Office when the security of the
country is at stake. The perception
has completely evaporated with Obama's
aggressive campaign to protect the
homeland. Republicans can no longer
claim monopoly in the security of the
country, and it shows. Even during the
2016 presidential campaigns, the
advantage Republicans usually enjoy -
*by simply mentioning their strength to
protect the country* - was virtually

non-existent. They had good reason not
to bring it up; Democrats would
quickly remind them it was Obama who
took care of the most notorious
criminal, Osama bin Laden, something
the Bush administration could not
accomplish.

Brussels Airport Attack Aftermath

Having lost the argument in regards to
the security and safety of the
homeland, the Republicans have moved
the pole again; the debate is no

longer a national issue. Republicans have now resorted to terrorism overseas as a way to downplay and question the president's effectiveness vis-à-vis terrorism and security. They blamed the president for the Paris attack; they blamed the president for the Brussels' Airport attack; they continue to blame the president for all acts of terrorism which occurred outside the United States. Interestingly, dozens of terrorist attempts here in the United States have been foiled due to Obama's aggressive policy on stamping out terrorism. Besides, there were well over a dozen terrorist attacks on US interests overseas during the Bush administration. Contrary to Republicans however, Democrats have always considered those situations as scenarios the country has to deal with regularly, as cost of having a presence across the World.

Obama has made the safety of the homeland a very high priority in his administration, and it shows. Since he's been in the Oval Office, there's been zero successful large and elaborate terrorist attack on US Soil.

Trump: Time to Get Tough

In "Time to Get Tough", Mr. Trump preaches nationalism but nowhere is it more obvious he knows very little about leading a country than he speaks about national security. If one were to be from another planet, one would think that Donald Trump is definitely the man to trust to bring an end to terrorism in general and peace to the world.

Mr. Trump claimed he is so effective on national security that he would have caught bin Laden before 9/11/2001 even happened; *"I would've been tougher on terrorism. Bin Laden would've been caught a long time ago, before he was ultimately caught, prior to the downing of the World Trade Center,"* speaking to an audience in Cleveland, Ohio.

That's not all. Mr. Trump boasted his prescience of the attacks on the US soils; to a crowd in Myrtle Beach, South Carolina, Mr. Trump declared *"I predicted Osama bin Laden … was coming in to do damage. … In my book, I predicted terrorism. I can feel it, like I can feel good location in real estate."* For the record, Trump didn't predict any such event. Much like everyone else who is concerned about safety, it is always expected that terrorism will hit the major financial cities in the world at one point or another; that's exactly what Mr. Trump mentioned in his book "The America We Deserve".

Here is below the excerpt Mr. Trump used to "flaunt" his prescience about the 9/11/2001 terror attacks in America, "*Instead of one looming crisis hanging over us, we face a bewildering series of smaller crises, flash points, standoffs, and hot spots. We're not playing the chess game to end all chess games anymore. We're playing tournament chess — one master against many rivals. One day we're all assured that Iraq is under control, the UN inspectors have done their work, everything's fine, not to worry. The next day the bombing begins. One day we're told that a shadowy figure with no fixed address named Osama bin-Laden is public enemy number one, and U.S. jetfighters lay waste to his camp in Afghanistan. He escapes back under some rock, and a few news cycles later it's on to a new enemy and new crisis. Dealing with many different countries at once may require many different strategies. But there isn't any excuse for the haphazard nature of our foreign policy. We don't have to reinvent the wheel for every new conflict."*

But what's most peculiar about Donald Trump's claims is 1) he completely ignores information which is readily available about the topic, and more often than not, he simply repeats what experts already concluded without mentioning the source, thus making it seem he is also smart 2) even in the face of public and currently debated information, he would abstain from giving credit to the appropriate individual such was in the case of the

killing of Osama bin Laden. In an
interview accorded to CNN Wolf Blitzer
in December 2012, Mr. Trump argued
with Wolf that Obama didn't deserve
any credit to having bin Laden killed.
In a Trump's world, no one but him
knows what's good for the country; no
one but him knows how to protect the
country; no one but him knows how to
keep everyone safe.

While it is widely recognized that Mr.
Trump's greatest and most lethal
weapon against terrorism is his mouth
– probably Twitter now – it is one's
hope that his business skills can be
of help as far as leading the
appropriate agencies (Homeland
Security & et al) to perform the duty
of ensuring the nation's security.

This page is intentionally left blank

ENERGY & CLIMATE CHANGE

From presidents Ronald Reagan to
George W. Bush, the issue of Climate
Change was reduced to a political ping
pong match. Although each one of the
administrations preceding Obama's
implemented some sort of policy to
deal with the threat of global warming
but none of his predecessors took the
issue seriously enough. Case in point,
the Bush (George W. Bush)
administration refused to get the
United States to abide by the Kyoto
Protocol, - *an international treaty
signed in 1997 in Kyoto, Japan which
would require member nations to reduce
their greenhouse gas emissions* -
citing economic setbacks (*providing no
specifics as to what those setbacks
were*) in the United States. However,

in February 2002, President George W. Bush set a voluntary "greenhouse gas emissions" target for the country to encourage companies to voluntarily report and reduce their greenhouse gas emissions…"

The "voluntary target" set by the Bush administration was simply window dressing; in the United States, corporate social responsibility has been at an all-time low. From Ronald Reagan to Obama today, the number of corporate scandals involving executives at the highest level of the organizations have not abated; every so often, major impact (*usually financial but also environmental and social*) to the country (*or a state or an area of the state*) has forced legislators in Washington to step in to rein in on corporate behavior.

As of the revision of this book, there was an ongoing hearing in Washington regarding Wells Fargo bad business practice towards its consumers (http://nyti.ms/2hWvc41), the gist of which consisted in Wells Fargo's executives opening some two million accounts in the consumers' names without their consent and knowledge; the practice contributed to padding the financial success of Wells Fargo, thus the ability to justify paying the executives responsible for the "genius marketing" over $100 million dollars in salary and bonuses all the while eliminating the jobs of well over 5,200 employees who were scapegoated for the scandal.

So, it was no consolation that the Bush administration set a "voluntary" greenhouse gas emissions target for businesses. Republicans have always denied the existence of climate

change; it was thus not surprising
that the Bush administration didn't
consider the reduction in gas emission
important; it was not a priority for
his administration. But in order to
please the Republicans and not anger
the scientific community, the Bush
administration left it up to the
companies which could impact the
environment to work towards reaching
the "voluntary" target. As you might
have already guessed, there was no
penalty for any company to choose to
ignore the matter altogether. But
worse was the fact that those
companies would not incur any penalty
if, instead of working towards
reducing gas emission, did instead
increase the output. Republicans'
argument is that climate change is a
hoax. Fox Opinion's hosts for instance
have claimed in many occasions that
the freezing temperature in the winter

time is proof that global warming does not exist. Just when you thought those geniuses at Fox couldn't outdo themselves!

What is climate change?

Weather is not climate change; most Republicans who oppose any effort to curb global warming have used the fact that it is cold during winter and it snows as proof that global warming is a hoax. The NASA website provides useful information regarding the two (*weather and climate change*) and explains the details of what climate change means to the world and how it would continue to affect the weather; you can read about it on the NASA website at http://go.nasa.gov/2igi3QH

It wasn't until Obama assumed office in 2009 that the issue of global warming/climate change took center stage along with healthcare. Barack Obama had proved to be a different president when it comes to the issue of climate change; he did not simply talk about it; he worked in collaboration with other world leaders to save the planet. As such, in December 12, 2015, with US leadership, representatives (*heads of states, scientists and* experts) of 195 nations

gathered in Paris, France and signed
an accord for the first time
committing to lowering planet-warming
greenhouse gas emissions, an effort
they all agreed will help curb (or
eliminate) the most drastic effects of
climate change.
While the wing of the Republican Party
has been playing footsie with the
millions of lives here in the United
States and billions across the world
which would inevitably be impacted by
such disaster, Obama had done what
future generations - *including the
very Republicans (who have opposed him
throughout his presidency) and their
offspring* - will be most thankful for.

The New York Time magazine penned an
article in 2013 labeling Obama the
Environmental President
(http://nym.ag/2itFIwF).

In addition to a sustaining campaign
to combat climate change which has
threatened our planet, the Obama
administration also dedicated
considerable resources to implement
his energy plan which encompassed
various elements: oil, wind energy,
solar power, etc. and of course
climate change.

In the 2008 presidential campaigns,
there was an
"uprising"
against the
idea of
limited
offshore
drilling,
the gist of
which was
the

implementation of an energy policy
which would not rely solely on oil
drilling and production but would also
include wind energy and solar power.

Then candidate Obama ran on the
platform to follow through with his
plan to implement comprehensive energy
policy if elected president but his
Republican challenger, John McCain
countered with "drill baby drill", a

complete repudiation of an energy plan which would factor climate change.

During his presidency, Obama had not only acted on the promise he made (*in regards to his energy plan*) but he had also raised fuel efficiency standards for cars and trucks to combat global warming; his Clean Power Energy plan had also helped cut carbon dioxide emissions from power plants. Politics aside, "Obama had done more for Clean Energy than you think" (http://bit.ly/2igj5wi) according to a September 2015 article in the "Scientific American" magazine.

It was difficult to assess whether Republicans' argument against Obama's energy policy had any merit; after all, Republicans were always against everything Obama. Regardless, Obama understood that damage to our planet is not a Democrat issue; it should concern every American citizen who wants to preserve the planet for the future generations.

It is near impossible to comprehend why any individual (or group) would go against a policy which would benefit mankind. Be it hatred for Obama or complete ignorance, the outcome for the country, for the world will most likely be the same when the impact of climate change begins to manifest. Even if scientist were wrong in regards to climate change, there would be no harm to err on the side of caution. Americans do not have the luxury of supporting their respective political Party on issues such as climate change which does not discriminate on the basis of political party; the future of our planet depends on everyone' collaboration and cooperation.

Trump's Open Mind

In a November 22, 2016 interview – that's weeks following the general election – accorded to New York Times, President Elect Trump suggested that he has an open mind regarding the issue, not to be believed. In a previous interview with MSNBC Chuck Todd in October 2015, Mr. Trump targeted EPA as one of the agencies he would eliminate as president. Besides, in the course of the interview, President Elect Trump made a number of statements which contradicted the "open mind" statement he made earlier in the interview with New York Times; here are briefly a few of his thoughts on the topic:

1.- "the hottest day ever was in 1890-something, 98." Mr. Trump wanted to point to the fact that the only hot day in winter (98-degree) was registered in 1890.

2.- climate change is a "very complex subject … I'm not sure anybody is ever going to really know." Well, the scientists know; there is a general consensus among scientists (97%) that global warming is indeed real and caused by human activity primarily.

3.- There is "some connectivity" between climate change and human activity, but it "depends on how much." Despite having refuted the possibility at first, here Mr. Trump posed as expert to suggest it cannot be as bad as the scientists suggest.

4.- The president-elect attempted to point to Climategate - http://www.factcheck.org/2009/12/climategate/ - as the reason he doesn't believe global warming is real.

It's not difficult at all to figure out where Mr. Trump stands on the issue, what's confusing however is to attempt to figure out whether Mr. Trump believes any of the things he says. 1) He didn't make any announcement about dismantling the agency responsible for study and research on climate and the environment 2) His appointment as Secretary of Energy, Rick Perry is someone who shares his belief on climate change and Rick too promised to dismantle the agency as candidate for president in the 2012 presidential election.

Whatever his reasoning, his decision NOT to eliminate the agency is welcome relief for the country; the EPA is not simply responsible for study & research on climate, the agency is also very important to monitor the water we drink, the air we breathe and to prevent callous corporations from dumping dangerous chemical in nearby

water system. EPA stands for
Environmental Protection Agency,
an agency of the Federal government
created for the purpose of protecting
human health and the environment by
writing and enforcing regulations
based on laws passed by Congress.
That's enough information to tell
anyone the agency is critically
important for the wellbeing of the
nation.

This page is intentionally left blank

HEALTHCARE

During his campaign in 2008 for the
presidency of the United States, Obama
promised to reform the healthcare
system; his goal was to have everyone
in America covered under some form of
universal healthcare system, much like
Canada, European countries and any
other developed country; that was one
of the few items in then candidate
Obama's check list if elected
president.

Having defeated Senator John McCain in
the general elections, Mr. Obama was
sworn into office in January 2009.
Upon assuming the presidency, Obama
made good on his campaign promise in

regards to the healthcare system; he
sent a comprehensive proposal to
Congress, known as the Patient
Protection and Affordable Care Act
(PPACA) but widely known and referred
to as Obamacare (*initially by
opponents to the healthcare act*). Both
Houses (*then led by Democrats*) gave
green light to the President's
Healthcare policy – *It is worth noting
that NOT a single Republican voted for
Obamacare* – and On March 23, 2010,
President Barack Obama signed the act
into law.

In a logical
world where
most people
could make
use of their
brains to
parse,

dissect and analyze information, Obamacare would be considered God sent for the nation but as you are most likely aware, the Republican constituents, led by their leaders in Washington (*the Representatives in both Houses*) and Powerbrokers across the nation, organized protests, spread rumors (*about the act*), propagated false information (*about its impact on seniors: individuals advanced in age*) and used scare tactics to mobilize as many Republicans across the nation to oppose the act. Sarah Palin, John McCain's running mate in the 2008 presidential election, – *famous for being able to see Russia from her living room in Alaska; she was also the former Governor of the state of Alaska* – spread the rumors that Obamacare would make use of a "Death Panel" for Seniors, the gist of which suggested that if you were a Senior and were not in good health, a panel of doctors would decide on whether you would be eligible to be treated back to good health or put to death, the raw version of which suggested that a group of doctors would decide on whether you live or die.

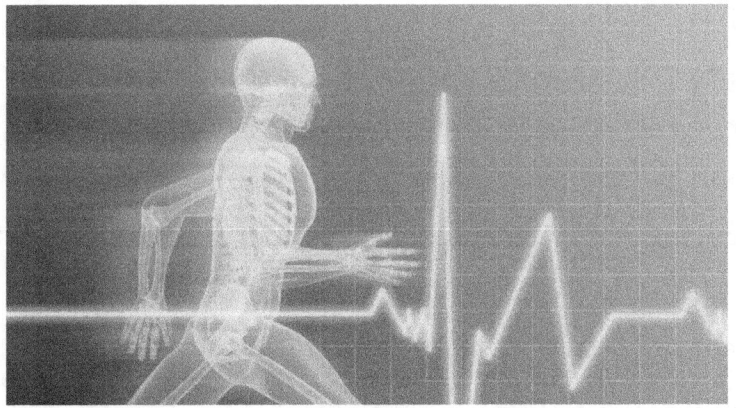

That would scare the living day out of anyone, especially those who are advanced in age, more prone to not enjoying good health. Any rational individual would debunk the rumor as nonsense; however, aided by its mouthpiece Fox Opinion – *known and referred to by most as Fox News* – and many other Republican broadcasting outlets (Limbaugh, Hewitt, etc.), the rumor took a life on its own and "Death Panel" was debated in every Republican circle as if it was true.

The Republican Party did a big disservice to its constituents; it misinformed them, it deceived them, it dragged them to protest against a policy which could benefit them greatly and thus made it extremely difficult (if not impossible) to improve and expand the healthcare act. Added to such fierce opposition to Obamacare by all Republicans, it didn't help Obama's cause that the website designed to accept registration into the program was not fully operational by the time the window for enrollment was opened.

Such fiasco added fuel to the rhetoric by the Republicans that the Obamacare program would also be a fiasco. - *It should be noted that president Obama did indeed drop the ball; it is difficult to understand that a policy which could define his legacy was left so vulnerable to those types of problems. Obama should have been more pro-active; he should have been more hands-on* - In addition to promoting the misleading premise that Obamacare would cost jobs to hundreds of thousands (if not millions) of people, the technical glitches on the enrollment site were used as example by Obamacare's opponents that if a simple task such as enrolling people into the program was met with so many difficulties, one could only imagine how much more difficult it would be for the participants to obtain

healthcare treatment after enrollment.
- *That was fair criticism; Obama
should have known better. He should
have been available, handholding the
individual responsible to get the site
ready for enrollment; Obama did indeed
drop the ball* - Republicans
capitalized on a problem that mostly
every new program would go through
regardless of the party which would
introduce such program. Amidst the
constant opposition by Republican
legislators who wanted to ensure that
Obamacare would indeed be a failure,
many Republican false prophets arose
to predict that the worst (about
Obamacare) was coming; here is in a
nutshell what they were saying:

John Boehner, 1/6/2011: "When you step
back and look at the totality of this,
I don't think it's ever going to
work."

John Boehner, 7/15/2012: "ObamaCare is only making our economy worse, driving up health costs and making it harder for small businesses to hire."

Victor Davis Hanson, National Review, 11/13/2013: "In the next 90 days, the Obama administration will have to declare victory and then abandon most of Obamacare. The legislation defies the laws of physics."

Bill Kristol, 11/3/2013: "Obamacare is failing and will fail. And I'm very much looking forward to being on this show [Meet the Press] with [David Axelrod] in January of 2017 when finally, all of Obamacare is repealed."

Rep. Paul Broun, 10/07/2013: "America is going to be destroyed by Obamacare, so whatever deal is put together must at least reschedule the implementation of Obamacare. This law is going to destroy America and everything in America, and we need to stop it."

Glenn Beck, 11/19/2009: "This is the end of prosperity in America forever, if this passes. This is the end of America as you know it."

Tom Coburn, 10/13/2010: "There will be no insurance industry left in three years. That is by design. You're going to make insurance unaffordable for everyone — which is what they want. Because if there's no private insurance left, what's left? Government-centered, government-run, single-payer health care."

Rush Limbaugh, 2/6/2014: "This is horrible for our country ... an

absolute tragedy ... It breaks my
heart folks to see this literal
tragedy happen to this country ...
Obamacare is going to cost this
country two and half million jobs
minimum."

Rand Paul, 2/20/2015: "I think that
what's going to come out of ObamaCare
is worse than anybody can imagine. I
think it will lead to bankruptcy in
the states that are fully embracing
it."

Scott Walker, 2/20/2015: "In a 2013
interview with CNBC's Larry Kudlow,
Wisconsin Governor Scott Walker argued
that Obamacare was hampering the
economic recovery."

            AND THEY WERE ALL WRONG!

Trump's War on Obamacare

Although Mr. Trump praised Obama in
the past and even suggested that
Obamacare was a good start to
implementing universal healthcare; as
a candidate however, the famous "I
will repeal Obamacare" statement
became a rallying theme for his crowd.
Although it's too early to know
whether he would carry out the threat
of repealing the Healthcare Act, it's
not even clear what that would mean in
reality since the Republicans do not
even have an alternative plan.

As of this writing, Obamacare has
survived, that is welcome news for the
millions of individuals who are
enrolled into the program. In spite of
the fierce opposition to the
healthcare act, a number of

individuals – *irrespective of their
political preferences* – must be
grateful for Obamacare; most notable
are the people who would have not been
able to acquire coverage, individuals
with pre-existing health conditions.
In addition, Obamacare has made it
possible for parents to continue to
provide coverage for their children up
to 26 years of age.

Those two aspects of the act alone
should have warranted widespread
acceptance by the constituency of all
political Partys. If nothing else,
Obamacare has now made it impossible
for any health insurance company to
deny coverage to any individual
because of a pre-existing health
condition.

It is important to note that prior to
Obamacare, most health insurance

companies had the practice of cancelling the coverage for anyone whose treatment was considered too expensive; but the insurance companies would mask the cancellation of the coverage under the guise of pre-existing conditions.

In most instances, the insurance companies would increase the premium so drastically it was impossible for the patient to keep up with the payment, thus forcing him/her to lose health coverage when s/he needed the most. And even those who could manage to pay the high premium were only partially covered up to a certain amount (*usually a low threshold set by the insurance company; there was no government regulation as to what that cap should be*) the patient would have to pay out of pocket for a major part of their healthcare treatment forcing

him/her to seek other financial
options to help cover the cost of
their treatments in case of a long
term illness. In all its shortcomings,
Obamacare is one of the most important
policy of the Obama administration.

Conclusion

What would Mr. Trump benefit for going
after Obama's achievements?

To satisfy his ego!

Mr. Trump is famous for holding
grudges and even more famous to wait
for or create opportunity to retaliate
against his "enemy". And Barack Obama
has been blacklisted by Trump as an
enemy.
Mr. Trump's vision is one dimensional;
although the statement might seem
subjective, suffice to take a walk
with Mr. Trump and try to convince him
of something he doesn't agree with or
doesn't believe in. There is no amount
of proof which will get him to
reconsider or even acknowledge to be
wrong.

Thus far, his ego has paid off; he is now the president of the United States. Although he didn't step into the position to create a legacy, he has one single focus: to destroy Obama's. Will he succeed? Can he even do that?

Well, each president creates (or has) a legacy irrespective of what other presidents do. A legacy is a historic event which does not depend on somebody else's input or action. As such, it is completely irrelevant what Mr. Trump decides to do regarding Obama's policies. He is simply creating his own legacy – whether he knows it or not -

About the author

Mike Ducheine born Michel J Ducheine of French descent, immigrated into the United States to study. Mike graduated with a Computer Sciences degree in 1999 and began a career in the field of technology. After a few years working for several organizations in various roles, – *from*

computer
engineer to
Chief Technology
Officer (CTO)
and Vice
President of
Strategy - Mike
returned to

school to obtain a degree in Business Management in 2003 at the University of California. Mike graduated cum laude with a 3.9/4.0 GPA. He pursued an MBA at the same school and graduated in 2005 with a 3.5 GPA.

At a very young age, Mike expressed a passion for reading and writing; at 17, he had already read the Bible three times from cover to cover. At the age of 18, Mike wrote a 100-page essay (in French) about the difficult assimilation of artificial organs into the human body. His insatiable thirst for knowledge and his passion for writing took him to pursue a degree in journalism and communication from the University of Massachusetts-Amherst where he graduated in 2014.

Mike spends his spare time publishing opinions and writing articles on The People Branch blog http://peoplebranch.org. Mike may be contacted via email (mducheiney@gmail.com) or via twitter @mducheiney.

www.ingramcontent.com/pod-product-compliance
Lightning Source LLC
Chambersburg PA
CBHW062126280526
45788CB00001B/74